Ecumenical Dialogue

ECUMENICAL DIALOGUE

Angelo Maffeis

Translated by
Lorelei F. Fuchs, SA

LITURGICAL PRESS
Collegeville, Minnesota

www.litpress.org

A title of the Unitas Books series published by the Liturgical Press.

Other titles available in the Unitas Books series:

Justification and the Future of the Ecumenical Movement: The Joint Declaration on the Doctrine of Justification William G. Rusch, ed.

I Believe, Despite Everything: Reflections of an Ecumenist Jean-Marie R. Tillard

Visible Church—Visible Unity: Ecumenical Ecclesiology and "The Great Tradition of the Church" Ola Tjørhom

Communio Sanctorum: *The Church as the Communion of Saints* Official German Catholic-Lutheran Dialogue

One with God: Salvation as Deification and Justification Veli-Matti Kärkkäinen

Cover design by Keith McCormick

This book was originally published in Italian under the title *Il dialogo ecumenico* by Editrice Queriniana, Brescia, Italy. © 2000 by Editrice Queriniana. All rights reserved.

1   2   3   4   5   6   7   8

Library of Congress Cataloging-in-Publication Data

Maffeis, Angelo, 1960–
    [Dialogo ecumenico. English]
    Ecumenical dialogue / Angelo Maffeis ; translated by Lorelei F. Fuchs.
        p.   cm.
    Summary: "Surveys the historical and theological foundations of the ecumenical movement; special attention is given to conciliar ecumenism and to the dialogues to which the Roman Catholic Church is partner"—Provided by publisher.
    Includes bibliographical references and index.
    ISBN-13: 978-0-8146-2931-4 (pbk. : alk. paper)
    ISBN-10: 0-8146-2931-8 (pbk. : alk. paper)
    1. Christian union—Catholic Church.   2. World Council of Churches.   3. Ecumenical movement.   I. Title.
    BX1784.M3413   2005
    280'.042—dc22

                                                                                    2004030302

Unitas Books

On the eve of his crucifixion, Jesus prayed that his followers "All may be one" (John 17:21). Christians believe that this promise is fulfilled in the church. The church is Christ's Body and his Body cannot be divided. And yet, the churches today live in contradiction to that promise. Churches that recognize in another Christian community an embodiment of the one church of Jesus Christ still too often find that they cannot live in true communion with them. This contradiction between the church's unity and its division has driven the ecumenical movement over the last century.

The pursuit of unity will require more than a few mutual adjustments among the churches. Ecumenism must involve true conversion, a conversion both of hearts and minds, of the will and the intellect. We all must learn to think in new ways about the teachings and practices of the church. Division has become deeply embedded in the everyday life and thought of the churches. Thinking beyond division will require a new outlook.

Unitas Books seeks to serve the rethinking that is a necessary part of the ecumenical movement. Some books in the series will directly address important topics of ecumenical discussion; others will chart and analyze the ecumenical movement itself. All will be concerned with the church's unity. Their authors will be ecumenical experts from a variety of Christian traditions, but the books will be written for a wider audience of interested clergy and laypersons. We hope they will be informative for the expert and the newcomer alike.

The unity we seek will be a gift of the Holy Spirit. The Spirit works through means, however, and one of the Spirit's means is careful theological reflection and articulate communication. We hope that this series may be used by the Spirit so that the unity won by Christ may be more fully visible "so that the world may believe" (John 17:21).

Norman A. Hjelm
Michael Root
William G. Rusch

The series editor responsible for this volume is William G. Rusch.

v

Contents

Introduction

Today, dialogue among the churches seems to be a self-evident given. Despite the state of separation in which they still are found and the difficulties involved in the search of mutual understanding and agreement, it is difficult to imagine other modes of relationship. This given seems less obvious when the whole history of the church is considered. It shows that dialogue has not at all been the only mode of relationship among the churches, and for long periods of time it was not the prevailing one. Historic events witness, in fact, to the presence of bitter controversies and religious wars, in some cases fought by armies but more often with weapons of theology. Even those that at first appear as periods of grace and tolerance among separate communities often hide a situation that is foreign and reflects an absence of communication.

Such a situation changed profoundly in the twentieth century with the emergence and the affirmation of the ecumenical movement, even though the incidence of cultural factors of a more general character cannot be denied. The expression "ecumenical movement" was affirmed as a synthetic designation of the whole initiative (doctrinal comparison, common social action, missionary cooperation, the creation of interconfessional bodies) that was promoted at different levels by members and leaders of Christian churches with the aim to overcome the historical divisions that occurred and to attain the visible unity of all those who confess faith in Christ. A priority was also to make every attempt to put the churches in dialogue to further their reconciliation, but almost always these were rather isolated episodes, and in general they were not able to prevent the logic of opposition that prevailed. The ecumenical movement has instead deeply altered the perception of other Christian communities in such a way that dialogue would be retained as the most suitable method for relationships among the churches and the privileged path to take in the search of unity.

This study intends to examine *ecumenical dialogue* as the fundamental mode of relationship among churches that, aware of the state of division in which they are found, intend to search for ways that allow them to overcome this anomalous situation. To explain the theme adequately, it would be necessary to introduce the whole history of the ecumenical movement and the problematics presently at the center of debate among the churches. The ecumenical movement, in fact, is nothing if not the whole of the initiatives, the instruments and the institutions that have as their purpose to let the divided churches enter into dialogue. "Ecumenical dialogue" then is a dimension present in all the expressions of the ecumenical movement, besides being the fundamental method adopted by the movement. Despite the difficulty to isolate the phenomenon of "dialogue" within the ecumenical movement as a whole, we would like to follow the theme in a narrow sense. Numerous introductions that present the history of the ecumenical movement and offer a review of the themes of current discussion are already available, even if they quickly grow old due to the progress of common work. What we would like to do instead is to retrace the stages of the history of the ecumenical movement in order to describe the processes that developed beginning from the moment in which the churches established contacts among themselves and undertook conversations, and to highlight the presuppositions and the implications of this praxis that in the passing of some decades became evident for all mainline Christian traditions.

In the *first part* (chapters 1–2), we propose to present some historical data related to our theme. We shall turn our attention to the development of the ecumenical movement that found expression in the World Council of Churches and to the evolution of the attitude of the Catholic Church that since the second half of the 1960s established many bilateral dialogues. The *second part* (chapters 3–4) intends to illustrate more systematically the constitutive elements and the principal dimensions of ecumenical dialogue: its scope, goals, methods, and the individuals involved.

Chapter 1

The Search of a Space for Dialogue

The ecumenical movement that developed in the twentieth century represents the privileged context in which the dialogue among the churches is affirmed and has gradually assumed more stable forms and structures. The ecumenical movement must not be thought of as a unitary phenomenon that from the beginning was precisely structured by the institutional point of view and in which all participants have shared the same vision of the pursued goals. On the contrary, in its first phases are found independent initiatives of a different character that for a relatively long time developed autonomously. Unity among these different initiatives results not so much from clear connections and bonds from the beginning, but from a retrospective look that assumes as its point of view the formation of the *World Council of Churches* (WCC), the body in which the different preexisting seams join. The assumption of this point of view, which lets us speak of ecumenical movement in the singular, is not, however, arbitrary. In fact, within the WCC, these initiatives reached a unity that is not reduced to the creation of a single depository for a heterogeneous reality, but that has guaranteed the coordination among the different ecumenical impulses and that has offered, however initial and imperfect, a manifestation of the communion among the churches that constitutes the final goal of all ecumenical endeavors.

The Beginnings of the Ecumenical Movement

The date and the place of birth of the contemporary ecumenical movement commonly coincide with the World Missionary Conference in Edinburgh in 1910. On that occasion, 1,200 delegates of missionary societies and churches (Protestants and Anglicans) gathered to compare themselves and to elaborate plans by which to continue their evangelizing activity in the world with renewed urgency. Section themes show that the debate of the conference concentrated on the urgency of missionary activity: the proclamation of the Gospel and the life of the church in mission lands; the meaning of the education in relationship to the Christianization of peoples according to their national peculiarities; the relationship between missionary proclamation and non-Christian religions; and the preparation of missionaries. Only the theme of the eighth section, devoted to "collaboration among the churches and the promotion of unity," had an explicit ecumenical intonation.

Despite this apparent marginality of the question of the unity of the church, the Edinburgh conference can be rightly considered as the beginning of the ecumenical movement for more than one reason. In the reflection on the strategies of mission, there emerges for the first time the consciousness that division among the churches constitutes the great obstacle that prevents the very efficacy of evangelization. In "mission lands," in fact, the different confessions often advanced their initiatives in mutual competition, with inevitable negative repercussion on the credibility and efficacy of Gospel proclamation. Precisely because it represented one of the circles in which the negative consequences of the division among the churches were felt in a most immediate and acute way, missionary activity also became the context in which the aspiration for unity began to reveal itself in a clearer and articulated form.

In the first place, the conference proposed an objective of a practical nature, that of creating the conditions for greater coordination of missionary initiatives so as to avoid overlapping of the different confessions and of mutual competition. Beyond this immediate objective of a practical order, it became obvious that reflection on the deep roots of such a situation could not avoid facing the issue of the division of the churches and to question what are the most appropriate ways to promote unity among the churches. Charles Brent, bishop of the (Protestant) Episcopal Church, who subsequently would be one of the prominent earlier figures of the ecumenical movement, insisted upon this in his intervention. From this point of view, besides the start of reflection on the ecumenical problem, the Edinburgh conference represented the place of encounter of some of the prominent figures who shaped the subsequent development of the ecumenical movement. Indeed, it can be said that for many of them this had been the occasion for discovering their personal "ecumenical vocation."

Given the predominantly Anglo-American character of the initiative, the immediate influence of the conference toward a growth in ecumenical awareness was not very notable, especially in Europe. Significant, however, for the consequences of the subsequent development of the ecumenical movement, is the fact that a committee entrusted to continue the work undertaken would be established. From this committee in 1921 is born the International Missionary Council that became part of WCC in 1961.[1] Since the beginning the ecumenical movement, therefore, evident is the tendency to go beyond occasional encounters devoted to the comparison of determined thematics toward the constitution of permanent bodies in which dialogue may develop with the greatest stability.

The *Life and Work* movement represents the second area that has contributed to lifting up dialogue among the churches in the beginning of the twentieth century. Born with the purpose of promoting collaboration among the churches on the practical level and in areas that do not involve dogmatic questions, the moving spirit behind this movement was the Swedish Lutheran bishop Nathan Söderblom. During the First World War he made himself the promoter of an appeal for peace which, he intended, would have to be undersigned by the churches. Even if at first the initiative had found a rather limited consensus and had involved only the churches of neutral countries, Söderblom had proposed his idea again at the end of the war: the churches cannot wait until they have reached full unity in faith and in church order to speak together on the most urgent problems of society and on the collaboration at the grassroots level. In particular, the weakness manifested by the churches during the war and the incapacity to speak with a single voice clearly showed the necessity to establish a united front in order to be able to intervene on international affairs and to promote peace.

The First World Conference on Life and Work met in Stockholm in August of 1925. Nothing new emerged in its discussion about the position of the churches regarding social problems. Rather, what had to be registered was a notable polarization within the Protestant churches between the position inspired by German Protestantism, which accented the distinction between ecclesial settings and secular settings, and the position of the churches of the Anglo-Saxon and French tradition that

---

[1] Cf. K. S. Latourette, "Ecumenical Bearings of the Missionary Movement and the International Missionary Council," chapter 8 in R. Rouse and S. C. Neill, eds., *A History of the Ecumenical Movement, 1517–1948* [Volume 1] (Geneva: World Council of Churches, 1993[4]) 351–402.

thought in more positive terms about the relationship between the kingdom of God and commitment to the transformation of society. In the first perspective, the kingdom is exclusively the work of God, and human activity cannot contribute in any way to its realization. In the second, human activity in society has positive meaning in relationship to the kingdom of God.

As it happened for the International Missionary Council, the Stockholm conference, too, sensed the need for a structure capable of assuring continuity in the work undertaken. To this end a committee was formed for the prosecution of the work that in 1930 was transformed into the World Council for Life and Work. The fundamental responsibility of the new body consisted in "promoting communion among the churches, affirming Christian ethics in relationship to the social problems of the modern life."

The story of Life and Work shows that the presence of the conditions so that the churches dialogue with each other in view of common witness and action in society was not entirely discounted. Before long the necessity surfaced to justify for what reason common action in the social field is founded on the very mission of the church and in what way such action can contribute to making church unity grow. The tacit presupposition of the movement, according to which "doctrine divides and service unites," is revealed in action a little more than a rhetorical affirmation, while it acknowledges that common action can only be born out of shared convictions about the nature and mission of the church. In the long run, therefore, doctrinal and ecclesiological matters cannot remain excluded from the dialogue set up among the churches.[2]

It is precisely in this setting that the attention turns to the *Faith and Order* movement that proposes to directly face existing doctrinal dissents among the churches in the formulation of faith and in church order. The movement finds its roots in the (Protestant) Episcopal Church USA, and in general reflects the American ecclesial climate characterized by an accented and growing fragmentation among the different confessions. In such a context, the Anglican tradition, particularly for its characteristic of being a *via media* between Catholicism and Protestantism, retains

[2] Cf. N. Karlström, "Movements for International Friendship and Life and Work, 1910–1925," chapter 11 in R. Rouse and S. C. Neill, eds., *A History of the Ecumenical Movement, 1517–1948* [Volume 1] (Geneva: World Council of Churches, 1993⁴) 507–42; N. Ehrenström, "Movements for International Friendship and Life and Work, 1925–1948," chapter 12 in R. Rouse and S. C. Neill, eds., *A History of the Ecumenical Movement, 1517–1948*, 543–96.

the ability to function as a meeting point and center of unification for the churches. Obviously, this does not mean pretending that the other churches assume all the characteristics proper to Anglican ecclesial life. Rather, it is individualized beyond the historically contingent elements, an "Anglican principle" summarized in the recognition of the four constitutive elements of the church and, therefore, necessary for its unity: the Holy Scriptures as the Word of God; the ancient Creeds as the rule of faith; the two Sacraments ordained by Christ himself; and the historic episcopate as the keystone of governmental unity.[3] At the foundation of the model is the conviction that these are the characteristic fundamental elements of the ancient church that can still represent a meeting point for different churches in the search of unity. This description of the unity of the church and of the essential elements it requires was made in 1886 by the General Convention of the (Protestant) Episcopal Church meeting in Chicago and the two years later by the bishops of the Anglican Communion gathered for the Third Lambeth Conference. From that moment it is known as the (Chicago-) Lambeth Quadrilateral.

At the beginning of the twentieth century, these ideas about the unity of the church issue from the setting of Anglican theology and are compared with other theological traditions and conceptions of the church. This happens at the initiative of Bishop Charles Brent who proposes to the (Protestant) Episcopal Church to create a commission with the task of preparing a conference in which it would be possible to reflect together with all Christian traditions that confess our Lord Jesus Christ, God and Savior, upon matters dealing with the faith and church order. The purpose of the projected conference will therefore be

> considering those things in which we differ, in the hope that a better understanding of divergent views of Faith and Order will result in a deepened desire for reunion and in official action on the part of the separate Communions themselves. It is the business of the Conference, not to take such official action, but to inspire it and to prepare the way for it.[4]

After a long and complex preparation, the project finds realization in the World Conference on Faith and Order held in Lausanne in 1927. As the experience of the preceding conferences taught, there was a

---

[3] Cf. W. R. Huntington, *The Church-Idea: An Essay towards Unity,* Boston, 1870, 155–57.
[4] *Report of the Committee on Plan and Scope adopted April 20, 1911* (Faith and Order Paper 3 [I series]), in *Joint Commission Appointed to Arrange for a World Conference on Faith and Order,* n.p.: n.p. 1911 (reprinted 1912) n. 1, p. 4.

notable distance between the desire to enter into dialogue and succeeding in doing so, and the creation of conditions for effective dialogue was not so easy. Difficulties were also accentuated by the fact that expectations of the conference participants were quite diverse, as different as the way of representing the objective of the initiative. For some, it was to serve to reach organic unity, based on the four elements of the Lambeth Quadrilateral. Others thought about a federation among the churches. Still others held that it was an occasion for each to present his or her own position concerning the unity of the church.

The method followed by the work foresaw the presentation of relationships from qualified representatives of the different confessions that illustrated the themes of the conference from the point of view of the respective confessional tradition. Doctrinal dialogue in this first phase essentially assumes the character of comparison among the ecclesiological conceptions in order to isolate points of dissent and points on which it is possible to register some convergence. If, therefore, Anglicans put on the table a conception of church unity that, in the intentions of its promoters, must serve as a possible point of convergence among the churches, in fact the conference reveals that the theological differences are still too deep to reach to delineate a common vision of the unity of the church and that it must limit itself to making inventory of the points of convergence and divergence.

A general look at the beginnings of the ecumenical movement reveals, among many characteristics, two that deserve to be pointed out. First, it can be observed how in its first phases it constitutes the *beginning of a dialogue* among the churches, with the hopes and the enthusiasm evoked by the enterprise, but also with all the difficulties and uncertainties that accompany the first steps on a journey that is risked upon unexplored territory. In fact, it is realized early on that, beyond subjective good will, to enter dialogue the churches must overcome the mutual foreignness amassed throughout the centuries and indeed must search for a common language that allows them to understand one another. To respond to such need the ecumenical movement is not concerned about constructing a new theory of theological language but has undertaken comparative study on concrete matters—mission, ethics, doctrine—in which the consequences of the division were experienced in particularly evident ways and which, therefore, could not be eluded. Acceptance of facing those who sustained different positions fractured the tranquility of many certainties that appeared obvious within one's own tradition. In fact, if dialogue does not press anyone to renounce personal convictions, it is equally true that it shows that it is not enough to claim having such a decisive or presumed answer to the matters at hand, but that it is necessary to create a consensus around it with reasoning that proves convincing to the interlocutors. This calls for a long and tedious journey.

Second, the beginnings of the ecumenical movement reveal the necessity to find *places of dialogue* in which the churches can communicate with each other. This is the significance of the tendency to give different initiatives a more stable form from an institutional point of view. In this way, in fact, dialogue loses its episodic and occasional character and assumes a more stable and binding character.

The Emergence of the World Council of Churches

After having gone part of the way separately, the movements mentioned contributed to the creation of the World Council of Churches that constitutes a first point of arrival and a more suitable institutional instrument to serve the ecumenical movement. The emergence of this new body represents the answer to the need to create a place for dialogue among the churches, characterized by greater stability and more binding adhesion on the part of the churches disposed to participate in it. The decision to form the WCC was immediately connected to affirming the conviction that the two movements, Life and Work and Faith and Order, must work together. In fact, in a clearer way, it is perceived that they represent partial approaches to the ecumenical problem and that their merging is not only desirable but necessary. The development of the reflection in Life and Work shows more and more evidently that the church's social commitment implies a vision of its mission and nature. In the long run, the exclusion of theological matters appears unsustainable, even if motivated by the intention to make practical collaboration possible. Likewise, the theological work of Faith and Order reveals that divisions among the churches do not depend only on theological controversies. They are linked to a whole series of nondoctrinal factors that throughout history have contributed in decisive ways to the verification of divisions, and even today they continue to prolong consequences of them. The need for a less restricted approach to the ecumenical problem that would integrate the perspective of practical collaboration and intense theological examination, is resolved with the will to create a more appropriate institutional scene for pursuing dialogue among the churches.

Thanks to the experience that matured in the first ecumenical conferences, the realization of an idea, symbolized for the first time in 1920
in an encyclical letter of the ecumenical patriarch of Constantinople,
became possible in the 1930s. Therein it was proposed to establish an
association *(koinonia)* that would gather the different churches and that
would pursue the goal of Christian unity, analogous to what happened
on the international level with the foundation of the League of Nations.[5]
Taken up and subsequently put forward again also by other exponents
of the ecumenical movement, the project was realized in 1937 when the
conferences of Life and Work and of Faith and Order decided to merge
the two movements in the formation of a World Council of Churches.
The outbreak of World War II forced a delay in the formation of the
WCC that took place in Amsterdam in 1948.

The WCC defines itself as "a fellowship of churches which accept our Lord Jesus Christ as God and Saviour."[6] In the definition of
its identity, the WCC makes its own the doctrinal basis already belonging to Faith and Order that also functions as the criterion for admitting
churches seeking membership in the council. If the Basis witnesses to
the bond with the early history of the ecumenical movement, it must
be observed, however, that, in comparison to the form the dialogue assumed in the first half of the twentieth century, it has made a qualitative
leap: we are no longer facing initiatives that see the participation of
individual exponents of mainline ecclesial traditions, but of a "council
of churches" founded upon the official adherence of the churches that
constitute it. In the act of its formation, the WCC expresses the intention
to be rooted in the life of the member churches that remain the parties
with the ultimate responsibility of their decisions and their initiatives.
The WCC offers these churches a place and a means for the common
search, since alone they are often incapable of making the journey toward unity and of establishing relationships with other churches. The
qualitative leap related to the nature of the institutional means at the
service of the ecumenical movement, however, also raises questions.
From the moment the parties that compose the WCC are churches,
what is the consequence of their uniting? Can an ecclesial character be

---

[5] The text of the encyclical letter is published in W. A. Visser 't Hooft, *The Genesis and Formation of the World Council of the Churches* (Geneva: World Council of Churches, 1987²) 94–97.

[6] W. A. Visser 't Hooft, ed., *The First Assembly of the World Council of Churches* (London: SCM Press, 1949) 197.

attributed to the entity that has been established? What "density" can be properly attributed to the possible ecclesiality of the council?

The answer given at Amsterdam in 1948 to these questions is indeed inspired by the intention to dispel some misunderstanding and to respond to objections raised regarding the WCC. This is evident in the preoccupation to state precisely what the WCC does not want to be. It is not a matter of a *super church* with a singular direction, nor of a great Christian church unified with a central authority that absorbs totally or partly the authority of the individual churches. The unity realized in the WCC does not correspond to the fullness of unity characteristic of the *Una Sancta,* nor is it understood as the last and definitive answer to the ecumenical problem.

Positively, with the WCC constitution it is affirmed that the new body, in virtue of the common confession of faith in Christ, is in relation with the unity that the churches intend to achieve and express in a fuller way. Reflecting on the meaning of the name chosen for the new body, General Secretary Willem Visser 't Hooft affirms:

> We are a Council of Churches, not the Council of *the* one undivided Church. Our name indicates our weakness and our shame before God, for there can be and there is finally only one Church of Christ on earth. Our plurality is a deep anomaly. But our name indicates also that we are aware of that situation, that we do not accept it passively, that we would move forward towards the manifestation of the One Holy Church. Our Council represents therefore an emergency solution—a stage on the road—a body living between the time of complete isolation of the churches from each other and the time—on earth or in heaven—when it will be visibly true that there is one Shepherd and one flock.[7]

The WCC thus understands itself as an instrument whose purpose is to serve the manifestation of the unity of the church. It, therefore, cannot consider itself the point of arrival. Its raison d'être lies in the dynamism directed toward the attainment of the unity of the church, and the common confession of faith in Christ placed at the foundation must be as the ferment within the life of the churches that increases their unity.

If the formation process of the WCC, in the narrow sense, with the meeting in Amsterdam and the approval of the constitution can be considered conclusive, there nevertheless still remain to be clarified numerous matters regarding the nature and the configuration of the WCC.

[7] W. A. Visser 't Hooft, ed., *The First Assembly,* 28–29.

Essential for understanding the nature of the WCC and the conditions in which its internal dialogue is to develop, clarification of such matters comes with the statement, *The Church, the Churches and the World Council of Churches,* approved by the Central Committee of the WCC in Toronto in 1950. This document traces the outline of affirmations of the Amsterdam assembly concerning the negative side (what the WCC is not) as well as the positive side (what the WCC wants to be).

It is not the intention of the WCC to become either a "super church" or a "world church." Neither is it the task of the WCC to directly conduct union negotiations of churches, because this prerogative belongs exclusively to the churches themselves. Not only does the WCC not impinge upon the autonomy of the actions of its member churches, it also fully respects their theological convictions. In fact, the WCC cannot and must not be founded upon a particular conception of church, nor does being a member of the WCC implicate that a church considers its own conception of church as relative or that it must modify its own judgment on the ecclesiality of other member churches: *"The member churches of the World Council consider the relationship of other churches to the Holy Catholic Church which the Creeds profess as a subject for mutual consideration. Nevertheless, membership does not imply that each church must regard the other member churches as churches in the true and full sense of the word."*[8]

The insistence to take distance from interpretations of the WCC that do not correspond to the intentions of its promoters does not have to darken the positive affirmations about the nature of the WCC contained in the document. The WCC founds itself on the conviction that dialogue, cooperation, and common witness among the churches are possible. Among common presuppositions that constitute the conditions of possibility of dialogue among the churches, the following are mentioned: the common recognition that Christ is the head of the ecclesial body; that the church of Christ is one; that belonging to the church of Christ is a fuller reality than belonging to any individual ecclesial body. Since they recognize in other churches the presence of elements of the true church, the member churches of the WCC feel obliged to enter dialogue with each other in the hope that such elements of truth can lead to the recognition of full truth and to unity based on full truth.

The image of the WCC that emerges from the Toronto Statement takes shape through tension. The *negative* side of the document affirms

---

[8] *The Church, the Churches and the World Council of Churches,* IV 4, in W. A. Visser 't Hooft, *The Genesis and Formation of the WCC,* 117. [Translator's note: citation is in italics.]

that the churches are approved as interlocutors in dialogue as they are, with respective theological convictions and without pressure that any of these would have to be renounced. However, the formula "ecclesiological neutrality" is used to describe the position assumed by the WCC toward the convictions concerning the nature of the church and of the ecclesial unity particular to the member churches. The formula is ambiguous and has been criticized. In fact, it could be understood as being indifferent toward ecclesiological matters, which would reduce the WCC to a simple instrument of collaboration among parties fixed in an unchangeable affirmation of their own identity, and so in reality denying the reason for which it was formed. Aside from the possible misunderstanding associated with the concept of ecclesiological neutrality, it is beyond doubt that the WCC could develop and gather the support of the churches that became members only on condition of assuring an absolute respect of their convictions about the nature of the church and the conditions necessary for its unity.

The *positive* side of the statement points out that this cannot be a "state" to preserve. Even when based on minimal but present elements that constitute a common ground of encounter, dialogue seeks to widen theological consensus and to deepen ecclesial communion. The point of departure is established in the consideration of the different conceptions of the unity of the church. The different visions are recognized as legitimate by the WCC, which nevertheless does not propose to simply preserve the status quo but to promote a dynamic directed toward unity through frank and loyal dialogue. The churches are taken as they are, but the aim is to bring them to converge toward a common point.

The "minimalist" position of the Toronto Statement elicits a certain surprise today due to what seems a scarcely binding character of connection with the WCC. The document must be understood in the historical context in which it matured and in relation to the finality of "ecclesiastical diplomacy" it follows. In fact, the statement was compiled with the intention to meet the difficulties of those churches that feared that connection with the WCC may require renunciation of their own convictions. It wanted to keep the door open to these churches that were observing the direction the WCC would assume. At the same time, the test of Toronto reflects a structural tension of ecumenical dialogue as such. On one hand, it is only possible because the parties of dialogue are recognized and accepted as they are, in their difference and, therefore, without asking them to renounce their own theological convictions and judgment that emerges from such convictions about the ecclesial quality of an interlocutor with whom they enter into dialogue. On the other hand, it is only authentic dialogue if a "parity" among interlocutors is recognized that cannot only be an expression of etiquette but implicates a recognition, at least incipient and partial, of the ecclesial quality of the interlocutor.

The noted tension leads to understanding the reasons for which the Toronto Statement—that today still remains extant—is an object of diametrically opposed evaluations. All recognize that it was necessary to pass through this phase in the beginnings of the WCC, because otherwise there would not have been the conditions to begin a common journey, but the fact that this situation persists is an object of conflicting evaluations. Already in the years immediately following the approval of the Toronto Statement, voices were raised that called for the overcoming of ecclesiological neutrality. Especially from the Protestant side, it has been underlined how the position assumed represents an excessive concession to the Orthodox and how it risks reducing the WCC to a simple forum for discussions deprived of any binding character. According to more radical critics, the fact that the Toronto Statement is still in use witnesses to the failure of the attempt made by the WCC to bring the churches to converge toward a common ecclesiological conception. Missing, in fact, is the courage to ask for the renunciation of their own conception of church to accept the common one the WCC has elaborated. They practically stopped at the point of departure.[9] More positive, however, is the Orthodox evaluation. The statement expresses the awareness of the WCC not to represent the last and definitive answer to the question of unity: it is a council ["consiglio"] of churches, not the council ["concilio"] of churches that manifests the one church and in which the mutual recognition as churches in the full sense finds expression in the common celebration of the Eucharist. Nevertheless, the picture defined by the Toronto Statement has not prevented the WCC to grow as a community of churches, both from the point of view of self-understanding and the point of view of the *koinonia* lived among the churches.[10]

---

[9] Cf. U. Duchrow, *Conflict over the Ecumenical Movement: Confessing Christ Today in the Universal Church* (Geneva: World Council of Churches, 1981) 306–12.

[10] Cf. V Borovoy, "The Ecclesiastical Significance of the WCC: The Legacy and Promise of Toronto," *Ecumenical Review* 40 (1988) 504–18.

The World Council of Churches Today

In the decades following its emergence, the World Council of Churches has welcomed numerous churches that were added to its founding members. While in 1948 it included 147 churches of 44 countries, by 1999 it included 336 churches from 120 countries. Moreover, it has developed an intense and manifold activity that grafts itself on to the historical roots that we have recalled, and has increased their measure. According to its constitution, the final goal of the WCC is "to call the churches to the goal of visible unity in one faith and in one eucharist fellowship expressed in worship and in common life in Christ, and to advance toward that unity in order that the world may believe."[11] This dimension is the particular focus of the activity of the Commission on Faith and Order, whose scope is to widen the theological consensus on the understanding of the church and its unity. Since the search for Christian unity is the primary task of the WCC and constitutes its raison d'être, the constitution underlines that all other initiatives and different sectors of action must relate to this fundamental goal.

The WCC intends then "to facilitate the common witness of the churches in each place and in all places" and "to support the churches in their worldwide missionary and evangelistic task."[12] Within the WCC the due importance given to the themes of witness, mission, and evangelization is not only a residue of the origins of the ecumenical movement that are tightly woven into the reflection on mission. It is more deeply a consequence of the conviction that the church is essentially missionary. The search for unity is, therefore, inseparable from the realization of the missionary mandate received from it and the condition for the effectiveness of Gospel witness.

The WCC also intends to serve the unity of the church through practical commitment in *diakonia*. In this way, it wants "to express the common concern of the churches in the service of human need, the breaking down of barriers between people, and the promotion of one human family in justice and peace."[13] Finally, to avoid ecumenical engagement being reduced to the management of "external" relations of the churches, the constitution emphasizes that the search of unity binds the churches to take up a journey that concerns their common identity

---

[11] Cf. Constitution of the WCC in M. Kinnamon, ed., *Signs of the Spirit: Official Report, Seventh Assembly, Canberra, Australia, 7–20 February 1991* (Geneva/Grand Rapids, Mich.: World Council of Churches/Eerdmans Publishing Company, 1991) 358.

[12] Ibid.

[13] Ibid.

and their way of existing. Through its service of the cause of unity, the WCC, therefore, also intends to contribute "to foster the renewal of the churches in unity, worship, mission and service."[14]

Besides the entrance of numerous churches from all continents into its membership during the fifty years of its life, the WCC has also been seen to deepen its collaboration with the Catholic Church, even though this church has not become a member of the council.[15] The success witnessed in the significant growth enjoyed by the WCC in the second half of the twentieth century, however, also introduces problematic aspects. In fact, not always does the reception of new parties correspond with a growth of consensus on the objectives to be pursued. On the contrary, the inclusion of new churches has contributed to the increase of differences in the ways to establish the priorities of the ecumenical movement. These problematic aspects readily emerged on the occasion of the fiftieth anniversary of the foundation of the WCC. For different reasons the recurrence has been remembered with tones all but self-celebrative. In addition to contingent factors, such as a difficult financial situation that forced a reorganization of the massive structure of activities, the "crisis" phase the WCC is currently going through comes from some deep-seated problems. These concern, on one hand, the adequacy of the structure for the purposes pursued, and, on the other hand, the loss of drive that seems to have struck the ecumenical movement on the whole. An honest and deep analysis of this situation was completed on the occasion of the fiftieth anniversary of the foundation of the WCC and in view of the Eighth World Assembly (Harare, December 1998) and has found expression in a document offered to the churches as a base for discussion.[16] The text represents a detailed "examination of conscience" that strives to single out the problems in view of relaunching the activity of the WCC. For this reason, it represents also for us a useful instrument for gathering the issues that the WCC finds itself facing and the choices it must make.

It is interesting to observe that, in this reflection, the terms already at the center of the debate at the time of the foundation of the WCC and on which the Toronto Statement had taken a position reemerge. It clearly deals with issues that cannot be evaded when it asks about the identity of the WCC. The actual resumption of the reflection on

[14] Ibid., 359.

[15] We shall return to the reasons for this choice in chapter 2.

[16] Cf. World Council of Churches, *Towards a Common Understanding and Vision of the World Council of Churches: A Policy Statement* (Geneva: World Council of Churches, 1997).

the identity of the WCC responds, therefore, on one hand, to the ever-present demand to renew the awareness of the shared aims that are at the foundation of the existence of the WCC, and, on the other, to the imposition of the changes taken place in the last decades that profoundly modified the ecclesial and world situation in comparison to the period of the foundation of the WCC.

The reflection on the aims of the institution and on the adequacy of the means used regarding the goal it intends to reach has been stimulated in the first place by the verification that the ecumenical movement has grown well beyond the confinements of the WCC, so much so that the council presently represents only a "part" of the movement. This fact inevitably raises questions about an entity defined as an instrument serving the ecumenical movement.

Besides growth in breadth, the demographic balance of the ecumenical movement also changed. While two-thirds of the churches that founded the WCC were European and North American, two-thirds of the churches presently members belong to the south. Moreover, it must be remembered that the churches with greater numerical growth are generally distant from the ecumenical movement (Evangelicals, Pentecostals, African Independent Churches). The document of 1998, therefore, acknowledges that there are ecclesial bodies that are not recognized in the WCC, evidently because they judge fidelity to their own convictions incompatible with adhesion to the council, or they hold the council to be a place not suited for the pursuit of the goals they hold as priorities for the church. The real possibility today is that, before too long, the WCC will represent only a minority of non-Roman Catholic Christianity.

The panorama of relationships among the churches has also been remarkably changed by the participation of the Catholic Church in the ecumenical movement and by the impulse it has given to bilateral dialogues. In addition, the formation of councils of churches and other ecumenical bodies on all levels, in which member churches of the WCC take part, has fostered an undeniable enrichment, but at the same time this involves the risk that these entities enter in competition with each other. In the end, the multiplication of bodies dealing with ecumenical matters seems to correspond with the diminution of the ecumenical impetus, with the consequence that the cause of unity impassions fewer and fewer people.

Added to these problems is that, among the member churches of the WCC, it is not rare to hear the complaint that the council has the

tendency to bureaucratization and, contradicting its nature, virtually
sets itself up as an autonomous party vis-à-vis the churches. In so doing, the WCC thus escapes the criticism that generally surrounds entities of central administration.

Since the WCC emerged as an institutional instrument in the service of the ecumenical movement, the changed situation presses for a
revision of the structures and a verification of their adequacy to the
purposes for which they have been created. Analysis of the situation
suggests two fundamental criteria that must inspire the revision of the
structure of the WCC: first, the inclusion of the greatest possible number
of entities active in the ecumenical movement; and, secondly, the elimi-
nation of the tendency to bureaucratization that makes the WCC self-
referential and modifies its nature as an instrument to serve the
churches. This is not just about matters of detail but concerns problems
that risk the very identity of the WCC and its self-understanding.

To answer the questions that emerge from the changed historical
and ecclesial situation, the document assumes as point of reference the
council's doctrinal basis that the churches expressly accept: "The World
Council of Churches is a fellowship of churches which confess the Lord
Jesus Christ as God and Saviour according to the Scriptures and therefore seek to fulfill together their common calling to the glory of the one
God, Father, Son and Holy Spirit."

Since the beginnings of the WCC, the expression "fellowship of
churches" has been subject to different interpretations that, despite steps
to resolve, continue to subsist. Some interpret the expression in the sense
that participation in the WCC permits the churches to discover essential
dimensions of their being church. In this line, it is added to affirm that
the communion *(fellowship)* realized in the WCC is a preliminary and
provisional expression of the unity in Christ the churches already possess today, or that in the common confession of faith, in witness, and
in service, a certain measure of the ecclesial *koinonia* of which the New
Testament speaks is already realized. For others, on the contrary, these
interpretations of the nature of the WCC go too far. Coherently, with the
original intention, the WCC must therefore remain an instrument at the
service of the churches to promote cooperation and mutual support. It
cannot in any way take the place of the churches themselves.

The existing differences do not prevent making some common
affirmations concerning the WCC. In such affirmations, the progress
made concerning the council's *ecclesiological neutrality,* claimed in the
Toronto Statement, can be recognized, as well as the consequent elabo-

ration of the minimal ecclesiology found in the positive affirmations of the statement. The fundamental conviction is that the WCC is essentially constituted by the dynamic reality of *relationships* among the member churches. At the foundation of such relationships is the recognition that the mutual commitment assumed by the churches through their participation in the WCC is rooted in the bond formed among them by the action of God in Jesus Christ and, therefore, represents a link that precedes and is deepened within that created by the decision to join the council. What defines the WCC's identity initially is nothing other than the complex of relationships of the churches among each other and the mutual commitment assumed by them to share the journey toward unity. If, therefore, belonging to the WCC does not impose a particular understanding of the nature of the *fellowship* lived within, the council offers a space to the churches for dialogue within which they can explore the meaning of their actual being in "communion" in view of a greater unity in Christ. From this conception of the nature of the WCC is also derived the priority of the relationships among the churches in comparison to the institutional reality: the WCC possesses a structure and an organization, but it cannot be identified with its structure.

Concerning the relationship between the WCC and other bodies of the ecumenical movement, after having noted that today active entities in this field are more numerous than in the past, the document points to the risk that they take in mutual competition. On one hand, the document insists upon the necessity that the WCC collaborates with these entities. But, on the other hand, it also proudly vindicates the peculiar character of ecclesial relationships realized within the council. In comparison to regional and local councils of churches, the WCC represents a unique place where the churches can gather ecumenically on a global level. This universal vocation is concretely realized through various specific functions: to coordinate efforts to assure the coherence of the one ecumenical movement; to mediate between conflicting sides; to speak on behalf of those who cannot make their own voice heard; and to maintain connections between local and global matters.

Since the WCC understands itself as an instrument serving the one ecumenical movement, its structures should lend themselves to establishing and deepening relationships with those churches open to ecumenical communion, but that for different reasons hold that they are not able to become members of the council. To realize this objective, a revision of the structures of the WCC and in particular of the world assembly, which constitutes its more authoritative body, has been proposed. The present form of the world assembly, in which delegates from the member churches of the WCC participate with voting rights, appears less and less adapted to realize the functions assigned to it by the constitution and that in fact have already been at least partly absorbed by the Central Committee. Due to the large number of participants, the assemblies are not even the appropriate place for deep reflection on theological matters. Also, for the sake of realizing in a more effective way the WCC's responsibility for the unity and coherence of the ecumenical movement within the council, a proposal has been made to substitute the world assembly with a Forum of Christian Churches and Ecumenical Organizations. The advantage of this new form comes from the fact that it would permit participation of churches that are not members of the WCC and other ecumenical bodies working at various levels. By and large, the idea of the Forum received approval, but the necessity of further close examination was also underlined.[17]

With the idea of the Forum, there emerged within the WCC a call for a looser structure that would not suffocate the primary reality of relationships among the churches, and that would fulfill the intention to involve settings of the ecumenical movement remaining outside the WCC and that are suspicious of too rigid ties. The intention to ensure greater inclusivity and coherence in the ecumenical movement that prompted the proposal is something to be shared without reservation. Nevertheless, it can be asked whether such a transformation would not accent the tendency to attenuate the ecclesial nature and to minimalize the binding character of relationships among the churches. The proposed Forum would, in fact, easily be able to assume a character closer to that of a theological congress than to a world assembly of churches.

---

[17] Section XII, "Proposal for a forum of Christian churches and ecumenical organizations" of the Report of Policy Reference Committee I states: "The eighth assembly encouraged the central committee of the WCC to continue the process of consultation with leaders of the various bodies who have expressed interest in the forum. . . . In affirming further work towards the goal of providing opportunity for a more effective, more sustaining, more inclusive network of relationships among churches and ecumenical organizations, the eighth assembly offered the following guidance to the central committee in this effort: a) the WCC needs to give careful consideration to the nature and scope of its role with other partners in working towards the initiation of the forum; b) there needs to be a clearly articulated distinction between the nature and purpose of the WCC and that of the forum; c) participation by churches in a forum should in no way be seen as comparable to the ecumenical accountability and commitment of ongoing membership in the WCC; . . ." Diane Kessler, ed., *Together on the Way: Official Report of the Eighth World Assembly of the World Council of Churches* (Geneva: World Council of Churches, 1999) 169.

The current situation, therefore, reveals a tension between two essentials not readily compatible. On one hand, the decisive element of the WCC is recognized in the relationships among the churches, and, therefore, in the communion, although not full, that has grown among the churches. On the other hand, the need to also make space for bodies that have not joined the WCC pushes toward a looser institution that nevertheless seems to carry with it also a lesser degree of attention to joining and less intensity in ecclesial communion lived within this entity.

The series of events we have recounted shows that, among the factors that determined change in the relationships among the churches during the twentieth century, the development of the ecumenical movement has been decisive. It has initially given voice to the aspiration for the unity of the church that manifested itself in different contexts, and it created the conditions by which such a search could take place together. The creation of the WCC in 1948 represents the more solid and elaborate response to the need for a space for dialogue, even if the structure of this body is permeated with unresolved tensions that are also connected to contemporary problems. The symptoms of crisis that manifest themselves today in the life of the WCC and caused the revision of its structure to be placed on the agenda indicate that, on one hand, it aspires to establish an anticipation of the "form" of unity to which the churches tend, and, on the other hand, it continues to be viewed as an "instrument" by which the churches are served. The necessity to specify the ecclesial consistency and tenacity of the dialogical space that the WCC has wished to be for the churches is thus revitalized.

New Interlocutors and
New Forms of Dialogue

In the first chapter we traced the steps of the formation of the World Council of Churches, a body created for the purpose of offering a space where the churches could enter into dialogue. The result of this process does not, however, correspond fully to the intentions of the initiators of the ecumenical movement: the WCC does not include all Christian churches, so that its intentional universality actually finds only partial realization. In fact, the creation of a space for dialogue among the churches has had as its negative outcome, for different reasons, the exclusion of some bodies. Such exclusion has been deliberate toward those groups of Christian derivation not recognized in the Basis of the WCC: confession of christological faith—subsequently widened in a trinitarian formulation—represents, therefore, the minimal condition for coming to the dialogue table. More interesting, however, is another phenomenon; that is, the self-exclusion of some ecclesial bodies which, although invited to participate, do not find the conditions for dialogue assured by the WCC acceptable or sufficient. At least by numerical standards, the most notable case is that of the Roman Catholic Church.

In this chapter, we will examine the reasons why the Catholic Church did not accept invitations to participate in the ecumenical conferences of the beginning of the twentieth century and the reasons that subsequently brought it to review its judgment on the ecumenical movement and to actively participate in it, but without becoming a member of the WCC. The journey of the Catholic Church deserves attention also because in the moment when it made its entry in the ecumenical movement, besides collaborating with the WCC, it initiated a new form of ecumenical activity, that of bilateral dialogue. Such a form of dialogue, which has developed parallel to the initiatives of the WCC, has also contributed to giving a more active ecumenical role to the confessional families with which the Catholic Church has entered into relationship, and which in turn have established bilateral contacts among themselves.

Reasons for Roman Catholic Absence

Within the Catholic Church the concern for the unity of the church does not represent a "newness" that is entirely linked to Vatican II. Rather, it constitutes a steady constancy of its whole history. This is documented in the appeals to unity renewed with insistence in different ages and the initiatives directed especially to the Oriental churches so that they may reestablish communion with the Roman See. Such attempts have known only partial success and have given origin to the Eastern Catholic churches.[1]

From the beginning of the twentieth century, a new element appears on the scene. The Catholic Church no longer has a relationship with only separated churches and Christian "dissidents" to whom it makes appeal that they return to communion with Rome, but it must also take a stand toward the ecumenical movement and the effort exerted to overcome ecclesial divisions by those who adhere to it. Among the different promoters of ecumenical initiatives, Faith and Order was the movement that had also tried more convincingly to get the participation of the Roman Catholic Church. Through an exchange of letters (1914–1915) between Robert Gardiner, Secretary of Faith and Order, and Cardinal Pietro Gasparri, Vatican Secretary of State, the Catholic Church had been informed on the objectives of the movement. In his answer, Gasparri, in the name of Pope Benedict XV, encouraged the organizers of the conference and wished them success; but he also clearly affirmed that such success could be achieved only through the union of all Christians with the Catholic Church. In 1919, during a trip to Europe undertaken to involve the churches of the continent in the planning of a world conference, the leaders of Faith and Order personally met Benedict XV, who welcomed them warmheartedly. Nevertheless, on

---

[1] Cf. W. de Vries, *Ortodossia e Cattolicesimo* (Brescia: Queriniana, 1983) 125–62.

this occasion the official declaration also reconfirmed the unavailability of the Catholics to participate in the conference.[2]

With the encyclical *Mortalium Animos* of Pius XI, published January 6, 1928, the Catholic Church made its first official pronouncement on the ecumenical movement. Even if the document does not expressly mention names, in "pan-Christians" and "non-Catholics," who, despite their differences in matters of faith, want to unite themselves and unite all Christians, it is not difficult to recognize the exponents of the ecumenical movement who in the years immediately preceding gave life to the conferences of Stockholm (1925) and Lausanne (1927). Pius XI intended to admonish Catholics not to let themselves be deceived by the fact that the purpose pursued by these initiatives might actually be good and shared by the Catholics.

> Nevertheless, when there is a question of fostering unity among Christians, it is easy for many to be misled by the apparent excellence of the object to be achieved. Is it not right, they ask, is it not the obvious duty of all who invoke the name of Christ to refrain from mutual reproaches and at last to be united in charity? [. . .] In reality, however, these fair and alluring words cloak a most grave error, subversive of the foundations of the Catholic faith.

> Conscious, therefore, of Our Apostolic office, which warns Us not to allow the flock of Christ to be led astray by harmful fallacies, We invoke your zeal, Venerable Brethren, to avert this evil.[3]

The encyclical does not deny that the search for the unity of the church is an enterprise worthy of approval, but it observes that "pernicious errors" pollute the method followed. Dissidents, in fact, deny that only one church of Christ exists, and they claim to recover it beginning with its historical fragments.

> For they hold that the unity of faith and government which is a note of the one true Church of Christ has up to the present time hardly ever existed, and does not exist today. They consider that unity is indeed to be desired

---

[2] Cf. T. Tatlow, "The World Conference on Faith and Order," chapter 9 in R. Rouse and S. C. Neill, eds., *A History of the Ecumenical Movement, 1517–1948*, 403–41. On the evolution of the position of the Catholic Church toward the ecumenical movement, cf. E. Fouilloux, "Il cammino dell'ecumenismo," in M. Guasco , E. Guerriero, e F. Traniello, eds., *Storia della Chiesa. XXIII. I Cattolici nel mondo contemporaneo (1922–1958)* (Cinisello Balsamo [MI]: Paoline, 1991) 495–516.

[3] Pius XI, P. P., *On Fostering True Religious Unity*, Encyclical Letter of Pope Pius XI, 1928 [Mortalium Animos; CTS Do111] (London: Catholic Truth Society, 1954) 11–12.

and may even, by co-operation and good will, be actually attained, but that meanwhile it must be regarded as a mere ideal.[4]

The search of unity founded upon a least common denominator of the expression of faith inevitably leads then to indifferentism and relativism: "How so great a variety of opinions can clear the way for the unity of the Church, We know not. That unity can arise only from one teaching authority, one law of belief, and one faith of Christians."[5] To the same result, indifferentism also finally leads to the attempt to found the unity of the church upon mutual love rather than upon consensus in faith.

Recognizable in the background of the encyclical is the classical ecclesiological reasoning developed in post-Tridentine apologetics: the only true church, the perfect society instituted by Christ, continues to exist under the successors of Peter; all those that have detached themselves from it must recognize it and return to it:

> Thus, Venerable Brethren, it is clear why this Apostolic See has never allowed its subjects to take part in the assemblies of non-Catholics. . . . There is but one way in which the unity of Christians may be fostered, and this is by furthering the return to the one true Church of Christ of those who are separated from it; for from that one true Church they have in the past fallen away.[6]

In this position assumed by the Catholic Church toward the ecumenical movement a perfect coherence can be ascertained between the doctrine of church unity and the practical attitude toward other churches of the ecumenical movement. On the level of ecclesiology, the church of Christ is identified with the Roman Catholic Church that in an exclusive way embodies essential attributes of the church of Christ. On the practical level, this conception of the church does not allow the recognition of separate communities as partners with which to establish dialogue. To these communities it is possible only to present the invitation to return in order to recover the unity preserved integrally by the Catholic Church, recognizing at best the good personal faith of individual Christians born and grown up in separated communities.

---

[4] Ibid., 14–15.

[5] Ibid., 19.

[6] Ibid., 21. [Translator's note: The English translation does not translate the Italian "l'infelice idea" (Latin: ab ea infeliciter descivere) of this text. See *Enchiridion delle Encicliche* 5, Pio XI (1922–1939) (Bologna: Edizioni Dehoniane Bologna, 1995) n. 235.]

The Malines Conversations

Despite an official stance that would consider the path of ecumenical collaboration as impassable, the Catholic Church at this time was involved in conversations with the Anglican Church, although not with official status. The occasion to undertake dialogue had been offered by an appeal to Christian unity made in 1920 by the bishops of the Anglican Communion gathered for the Lambeth Conference.[7] In this appeal, the bishops declared themselves ready, in case Anglican orders would not be judged valid by some churches, to receive a form of order or of recognition from the authorities of these churches, if such was held necessary for the reestablishment of Christian unity. The affirmation is situated in a very particular context. It refers to the discussions going on in Great Britain with the Free churches and does not directly refer to taking the position of Leo XIII in the bull *Apostolicae Curae* (1896) in which Anglican orders were declared null and void. In the event of union with these Free churches, Anglicans demanded a regularization of ministers of the Free churches by Anglican bishops. In the document, they declared themselves equally prepared, if necessary, to an analogous regularization completed on the part of the authority of the Presbyterian and Congregational churches. Based on an extensive interpretation of the principle enunciated in the appeal, Lord Halifax saw an opening to the possibility of reconnecting the threads of the dialogue established with the French Vincentian priest Ferdinand Portal at the end of the nineteenth century. On the Catholic side, a major role in the resumption of contacts was played by Cardinal Désiré Mercier, archbishop of Malines.

The Malines Conversations consisted of five meetings from 1921 to 1926. They were interrupted after the death of Cardinal Mercier (1926) due to the stiffening of the Catholic English hierarchy and of the archbishop of Canterbury who made little of the conditions for continuing the dialogue. The conversations did not have as their goal to negotiate the reunification of Rome and Canterbury. Even if the respective ecclesial authorities were informed of the initiative, the members of the two delegations had no mandate to conduct a negotiation of that kind. On the contrary, theirs was a private initiative established to make a contribution to the clarification of the theological issues upon which

[7] Cf. "An Appeal to All Christian People from the Bishops Assembled in the Lambeth Conference of 1920," in G.K.A. Bell, *Documents on Christian Unity* I (1920–1924) (London: Oxford University Press, 1924) 4.

dissent was recorded between the two traditions in order to come to greater mutual understanding. Work was devoted to the close examination of themes of a historical-theological character: the differences in ecclesiology and in the doctrine of the sacraments; the disciplinary and juridical concessions that Rome would be disposed to make to the Anglican Communion once communion with the Holy See would be reestablished; the position of Peter in the early church and the authority of the pope.

The Malines Conversations did not change relationships between the Catholic Church and the Anglican Communion in any substantial way. Nevertheless, they cannot be judged insignificant. The very fact that they took place shows that for the Catholic Church it is also possible to enter into dialogue with other ecclesial communities without denying its own convictions. As to the form the dialogue took, the conversations provided a first model that would serve as an example for future ecumenical encounters. Historians and theologians with a specific competence on the matters dealt with entered into dialogue in Malines. Furthermore, although it was a private group, the members enjoyed some approval of the ecclesiastical authorities who showed at least a certain interest in common theological work carried out with the intention to prepare the way toward unity. This and other initiatives undertaken by ecumenism's "pioneers" ultimately allowed the Catholic Church, which at this time did not participate in ecumenical activities, to overcome its total estrangement from the ecumenical movement, and they created the foundation for the development of official contacts with other confessions after the Second Vatican Council.[8]

Vatican II

The shift in the Catholic attitude toward the ecumenical movement took place with the Second Vatican Council (1962–1965), even if the change of position is not understood without referring to the hidden action of pioneers of Catholic ecumenism who prepared the ground while the official stance remained cautious.[9]

[8] On the Malines Conversations, cf. John A. Dick, *The Malines Conversations Revisited* (Bibliotheca Ephemeridum Theologicarum Lovaniensium 85) (Leuven/Louvain, Belgium: Leuven University Press/Presses Universitaires de Louvain (Uitgeverij Peeters), 1989); G.K.A. Bell, *Christian Unity: The Anglican Position* (London: Hodder & Stoughton, 1948) 67–77; G. Tavard, *Petite histoire du mouvement oecuménique* (Paris: Fleurus, 1960) 122–32.

[9] Through the celebration of the Week of Prayer for Christian Unity, introduced by P. Wattson and renewed by P. Couturier, and other initiatives directed to make other

Vatican II welcomed a different evaluation of the ecumenical movement, especially for the renewed vision of the church delineated in the conciliar texts. Even before its explicit affirmations about ecumenism, therefore, the council is significant for the proposed ecclesiological concession that represents the presupposition of Catholic participation in the ecumenical movement. Decisive under this aspect are the affirmations in article 8 of the Dogmatic Constitution on the Church, *Lumen Gentium*, where it is declared that the church of Christ "subsists in the catholic church," but it also recognizes outside it the existence of "elements of sanctification and of truth" that constitute the basis of a real although imperfect communion with other churches and ecclesial communities.

> This is the unique church of Christ, which in the creed we profess to be one, holy, catholic and apostolic. After his resurrection our saviour gave the church to Peter to feed (see Jn 21,17), and to him and the other apostles he committed the church to be governed and spread (see Mt 28, 18ff.); and he set it up for all time as the pillar and foundation of the truth (1 Tm 3, 15). This church, set up and organised in this world as a society, subsists in the catholic church, governed by the successor of Peter and the bishops in communion with him, although outside its structure many elements of sanctification and of truth are to be found which, as proper gifts to the church of Christ, impel toward catholic unity (*LG* 8).

The section quoted has undergone divergent interpretations, partly because the council did not explain the exact meaning of the expression *"subsistit in."* In one sense, there are interpretations that do not see in the text any substantial freshness in comparison to the preceding ecclesiological conception. Thus, there is the conclusion that a unique subsistence of the church of Christ exists in the Catholic Church. At the opposite extreme, there is the thesis of those who hold that there are many subsistences of the church of Christ which are the churches that have been historically formed. Both interpretations appear problematic. If the intention of the conciliar assembly had been to affirm that there is only one realization of the church of Christ, the reason why the formula "the church of Christ *is* the Catholic Church" was changed to "the church of Christ *subsists in* the catholic church" is not under-

---

Christian confessions known to Catholics, awareness of the ecumenical problem also spread in the Catholic world. For the French setting, cf. the detailed study of E. Fouilloux, *Les catholiques et l'unité chrétienne du XIXe siècle. Itinéraires européens d'expression française* (Paris: Centurion, 1982).

stood. The change introduced in the conclusive phase of editing the text manifests without a trace of doubt the will to overcome an exclusive identification between the church of Christ and the Catholic Church. Equally evident, however, is the intention to affirm that the Catholic Church represents the historic place where the church of Christ is present and continues to exist with all the essential properties and with the fullness of the means of salvation with which Christ has endowed it.[10] This means that, if it must also recognize the presence of "elements of sanctification and of truth" outside the Catholic Church, it is not, according to Vatican II, however, possible to affirm that all the historical realizations of the church are in principle equivalent.

The consequences of these affirmations for the evolution of the Catholic Church's attitude toward the ecumenical movement are evident. To understand the course of the turn of events, it is enough to consider the doctrine of the first schema of the constitution on the church in which the dominant ecclesiological perspective is one that necessarily leads to a conception of ecumenism as a return to Rome.[11] The new element in the final text of *Lumen Gentium* is given by the fact that the identity between the Catholic Church and the church of Christ is maintained but not in exclusive form. The simplifying logic that opposes the presence or the absence of the church of Christ—belonging at least to the Body of Christ, identified with the juridical concreteness of the Catholic Church—is replaced with a schema. This schema is based on the idea of *fullness* that allows for the distinction between the *full* realization of the church and *partial and imperfect* realizations that nevertheless are not deprived of consistence and theological meaning. The ecclesial character of these communities derives from the presence of the "elements of sanctification and of truth" that belong to the church of

[10] Cf. F. A. Sullivan, "In che senso la Chiesa di Cristo 'sussiste' nella Chiesa cattolica romana?" R. Latourelle, ed., *Vaticano II: bilancio e propettive venticinque anni dopo (1962–1987)*, II (Assisi: Cittadella, 1987) 811–24. [Translator's note: An English version of this is "The One Church of Christ 'Subsists' in the Catholic Church," chapter 2 in Francis A. Sullivan, s.j., *The Church We Believe In: One, Holy, Catholic and Apostolic* (Mahwah, N.J.: Paulist Press, 1988) 22–33.]

[11] In the first draft, *De ecclesia*, distributed by the council fathers November 23, 1962, one reads: "The Holy Synod teaches and solemnly professes that there is but only one true church of Christ, that is the one that in the symbol we say one, holy, catholic and apostolic, that the Savior is gained on the cross and that one who has united to him as the body is to the head and as the bride is to the bridegroom and that after his resurrection entrusted Peter and his successors who are the Roman Pontiffs and that therefore only the Roman Catholic Church can rightfully be called Church," *Acta Synodalia Sacrosancti Concilii Oecumenici Vaticani II*, I/4 (Roma: Typis PoliglottisVaticanis, 1971) 15.

Christ operative in them. Such elements, then, exist beyond the Catholic Church not only in a state of "dispersion," but are organically connected among themselves and form what Vatican II defines "churches and ecclesial communities."

The ecumenical implications of this vision of the church are developed by the decree *Unitatis Redintegratio*. After having recalled the constitutive elements of the unity of the church, the decree illustrates the relationships of the Catholic Church with the Christians belonging to other confessions and affirms that "those who believe in Christ and have been truly baptised are in some kind of communion with the Catholic church, even though this communion is imperfect" (*UR* 3). Such judgment is not limited to baptized individuals but also extends to the ecclesial communities to which they belong.

> Moreover some, and even most, of the significant elements and endowments which together go to build up and give life to the church itself, can exist outside the visible boundaries of the catholic church: the written word of God; the life of grace; faith, hope and charity, with the other interior gifts of the holy Spirit, and visible elements too. All of these, coming from Christ and leading back to Christ, properly belong to the one church of Christ.
>
> Our separated brothers and sisters also celebrate many sacred actions of the christian religion. These most certainly can truly engender a life of grace in ways that vary according to the condition of each church or community, and must be held capable of giving access to that communion in which is salvation. It follows that the separate churches and communities as such, though we believe them to be deficient in some respects, have by no means been deprived of significance and importance in the mystery of salvation. For the Spirit of Christ has not refrained from using them as means of salvation whose efficacy comes from that fullness of grace and truth which has been entrusted to the catholic church (*UR* 3).

The texts quoted show with a clarity that a deep revision of judgment on the non-Catholic communities was made, with the consequence to overcome a vision focused exclusively on a negative moment of refusal, of difference. In fact, the historical separations have not completely destroyed the common patrimony of faith. Non-Catholic communities also derive their identity and live off the authentically Christian patrimony that continues to be present in them. Their historical existence, therefore, cannot be reduced to a "no" which they pronounce against determined doctrines or ecclesial structures, but is founded upon a "yes" to the essential elements of the common patrimony of Christian faith in virtue of which they exist as "churches and ecclesial communities."

Beyond its conception of the church, Vatican II also represented a change regarding concrete relationships with other churches and Christian confessions. The insistence on the range of the change of ecclesiological perspective need not lead to thinking that dialogue was set up simply as a consequence "deduced" from the change of theory on the church. In reality the renewal of the vision of the church promoted by the council and the opening of dialogue with other churches have gone on as companion movements, and between the two developments there has been a mutual influence. On one hand, a nonexclusive identification of the Catholic Church with the church of Christ has created conditions for overcoming the conception of church unity that was translated into the appeal to return to Rome. On the other hand, the effective relations established with representatives of other Christian confessions and the direct participation in the movement have led to reconsideration of many diffused ideas within Catholicism about other churches.

The figure of John XXIII, who has played a determining role in the evolution of the Catholic attitude toward other churches, clearly documents the precedence of dialogical opening in the revision of ecclesiology. Since the beginning of his pontificate, he showed interest in the question of the unity of Christians, and he devoted a section to the ecumenical problem in his programmatic encyclical *Ad Petri Cathedram* (June 29, 1959). Since he established an appreciable sympathy toward the Catholic Church and an increasing respect for the Holy See,[12] John XXIII felt encouraged to renew his appeal to unity:

> May We, in fond anticipation, address you as sons and brethren? May We hope with a father's love for your return? [. . .] When We fondly call you to the unity of the Church, please observe that We are not inviting you to a strange home, but to your own, to the abode of your forefathers.[13]

---

[12] "We are already aware . . . that many of the communities that are separated from the See of Blessed Peter have recently shown some inclination toward the Catholic faith and its teachings. They have manifested a high regard for this Apostolic See and an esteem which grows greater from day to day as devotion to truth overcomes earlier misconceptions. We have taken note that almost all those who are adorned with the name of Christian even though separated from Us and from one another have sought to forge bonds of unity by means of many congresses and by establishing councils. This is evidence that they are moved by an intense desire for unity of some kind," *Ad Petri Cathedram* 63, 64; [from the website of the Vatican, www.vatican.va].

[13] Ibid., 80, 84.

From the point of view of content, the conception of the unity of the church implied in the appeal is no different from that of preceding pontifical documents: the journey of unity coincides with that of a return to communion with Rome. Yet, what is new is the way in which the appeal of unity is presented to non-Catholic Christians. A cordial tone, deprived of arrogance, together with the personal style assumed by John XXIII in the exercise of his office, gives greater credibility to the desire of unity demonstrated by the pope.

The will to motivate the cause of unity was already expressed in January 1959 at the time of the announcement of the Second Vatican Council. On that occasion the pope had also presented to non-Catholic Christians the invitation to seek together the unity of grace passionately desired by many individuals from all ends of the earth. The announcement of the council and the fact that an ecumenical role would also be attributed to it aroused, along with high expectations, some misunderstanding. In fact, outside the Catholic Church it was thought by some that the qualification *ecumenical* given to the council was understood in the sense of an assembly that must gather representatives of all the churches to discuss Christian unity. The misunderstanding soon passed, but it is nonetheless indicative of an expectation so alive, and of a hope to garner a freshness in the Catholic Church's attitude toward the ecumenical movement.

It was necessary to create adequate means to translate into action the ecumenical role given the council. In fact, up to this time, Catholic absence from the ecumenical movement had prevented the creation of structures that would deal with the relations with other churches and with ecumenical organizations. At the initiative of the archbishop of Paderborn, L. Jaeger, the idea began to take shape to create in Rome a group of experts, with a press office, who would assume official responsibility for ecumenical affairs. The task was given to Cardinal A. Bea, who took the necessary steps with John XXIII. In March 1960 the establishment of the *Secretariat for Promoting Christian Unity* was established, and the same Cardinal Bea was named president. In June of the same year, the Secretariat for Christian Unity was officially established as one of the preparatory commissions of the council.[14] In the first place, this group was entrusted with the task to take care of the ecumenical

---

[14] Cf. M. Velati, *Una difficile transizione. Il cattolicesimo tra unionismo ed ecumenismo (1952–1964)* (Bologna: Il Mulino, 1996) 175–204.

aspects of the council. As a matter of fact, despite attempts made in some circles of the Roman Curia to reduce its meaning to a simple press office for non-Catholics, the Secretariat for Christian Unity acquired an active and motivating role during the conciliar proceedings, not only in the preparation of the Decree on Ecumenism but also in its constant attention to the ecumenical implications of the themes treated in other documents.

Furthermore, the Secretariat for Christian Unity assumed on the Catholic side the function of official interlocutor in ecumenical relations. In this capacity, the most immediate task to accomplish was that of exploring ways in which non-Catholic Christians could follow the council. To this end, the experience of Vatican I was not quite encouraging. In 1868 Pius IX had sent a letter to the "bishops of the churches of the Oriental rite which are not in communion with the Apostolic See" in which he implored them to participate in the council, as their fathers went to the Councils of Lyons (1274) and Florence (1438–1442), so that the peace accorded at that time might once again be operative. The invitation, however, was not followed up, due to rooted fears of Orthodox bishops toward Roman imperialism and because of the lack of tact with which the invitation had been expressed. In particular, the Orthodox bishops complained of the fact that the letter personally addressed to them had been published in Roman newspapers some weeks before and that it had been delivered to them, without any official form, from Latin missionaries who worked there. Nor did the appeal addressed to Protestants fare any better, as it called for their return to communion with Rome. Putting aside strong polemical reactions recorded in Germany, this fell into general indifference.

To avoid errors that could have jeopardized the success of the initiative, the Secretariat for Promoting Christian Unity tried to establish informal contacts with proponents of some churches and ecumenical organizations. Of particular importance was the secret meeting that took place in September 1960 between Cardinal Bea and the Secretary General of the WCC, W. A. Visser 't Hooft. The president of the Secretariat for Promoting Christian Unity hoped to confidentially verify an interest on the part of the member churches of the WCC to receive invitations to attend the council as observers. The reaction of the Secretary General was positive, and he assured the availability of his organization to help the Catholic Church to establish contacts with the churches. Also discussed in the meeting was the possibility of the presence of Catholic observers to the world assembly of the WCC that was to take place in 1961 in New Delhi.[15] In this phase, of fundamental importance was the network of personal relationships with the proponents of the ecumenical movement that the "pioneers" of Catholic ecumenism had developed during the times when the Catholic position was cautious. Noteworthy is the example of J. Willebrands, who, from secretary of the Catholic Conference for Ecumenical Questions, became secretary of the Secretariat for Christian Unity, but the personnel and consulters of the Secretariat were in general chosen from the Catholic ecumenical circles that had prepared the ground in the preceding decades.

In the meantime, the issue of the opportunity and the formalities of the possible invitation of non-Catholic observers at Vatican II was also treated in the Central Preparatory Commission.[16] This office defined the identity of the observers, recognizing their status as official delegates of the respective churches and ecumenical entities that had sent them. As such, they could participate in the general sessions; they received all the material distributed to the council fathers; they had access to all information and could freely inform the churches and ecclesial communities they represented. The fact that the observers had direct access to the information about the unfolding of the conciliar workings allowed them to inform the churches they represented with precision, enabling them prepare firsthand information.

During the periods when the council met, an intense dialogue was established between the observers and the members of the Secretariat for Promoting Christian Unity, above all through weekly meetings in which were treated the themes that were the subjects of the conciliar discussion at that moment. In the encounters organized by the Secretariat and in other informal occasions, the observers had the possibility to meet numerous council fathers and experts [periti] and to exchange with them their opinions and observations relative to the development of the conciliar proceedings. Through these exchanges, the observers were able to represent the point of view of the respective traditions and had exercised a certain influence, even though indirect and mediate through the fathers and experts, on the editing of the conciliar documents.

Through the presence of observers at Vatican II, a "discovery" of the Catholic Church by other churches took place. The vivacity of the conciliar discussion revealed a sincere desire of ecclesial renewal to-

---

[15] Cf. A. Bea, *Ecumenism in Focus* (London: Geoffrey Chapman, 1969) 28–41; W. A. Visser 't Hooft, Memoirs (Geneva: World Council of Churches, 1987²) 328–30.

[16] Cf. *Acta et Documenta Concilio Oecumenico Vaticano II Apparando*, Series II (Praeparatoria), II/1 (Roma: Typis Polyglottis Vaticanis, 1965) 427–36, 449–95.

gether with the presence of differentiated positions, thereby consenting to overcoming of many prejudices fed by deficient knowledge. In this way, Vatican II was an event whose importance was not limited to the Catholic Church alone but to a certain degree involved all the churches. This is affirmed by the observers themselves in the message addressed to the council fathers on December 4, 1965, at the end of the council.

> We have been invited, so that assisting the work of the council, we could know about it more profoundly and could inform our churches about it. We have always been welcomed with exquisite cordiality. We have received countless gestures of respect, of charity and of friendship. Dialogue, which was spoken of often, has not remained empty and dead words. . . . At this time we desire to assure the council fathers of only one thing, and that is that we have followed the work of the council not merely with the attention of a detached spectator, but with a sense of real participation. In fact, how much takes place within one church also interests all the others. Despite the divisions, the churches stay nevertheless united in the name of Christ. We observers are firmly convinced that the communion which has been reached up to this moment can still grow and that it surely will grow.[17]

Relationships with the World Council of Churches

Vatican II clarified the ecclesiological foundations for Catholic participation in the ecumenical movement and, through the presence of observers, marked the beginning of a dialogue between the Catholic Church and other Christian churches. After the conciliar assembly, there arose the problem to personalize the concrete formalities to develop the contacts established through the observers in a more stable and organic way and to carry out the directives contained in the Decree on Ecumenism about the dialogues to be set up with other churches and ecclesial communities. In the postconciliar period, the ecumenical activity of the Catholic Church is mainly developed in two directions. First, collaboration is undertaken with the World Council of Churches that represented the most important institutional expression of the ecumenical movement emerging at the beginning of the twentieth century. Second, numerous bilateral dialogues with mainline churches and confessional families were set up. Before describing the forms of ecumenical

---

[17] *Acta Synodalia Sacrosancti Concilii Oecumenici Vaticani II*, IV/1, 56, §22.

collaboration and the initiatives of dialogue more analytically, it must be remembered that the new position assumed by the Catholic Church created an unprecedented situation for the ecumenical movement as a whole. If, in fact, the WCC had first had the almost exclusive monopoly of ecumenical activity, now it found itself facing another body of non-negligible dimensions that would have forced the WCC to redefine its own identity.

Collaboration between the Catholic Church and the WCC developed on different levels. In 1965 the *Joint Working Group between the Roman Catholic Church and the World Council of Churches (JWG)* was established with the task to examine the possibility of dialogue and collaboration. The Joint Working Group does not have deliberative power but is limited to examine problems of common interest, transmitting to the respective authorities the conclusions of their work. From the moment of its constitution until today, the activity of the JWG is mainly developed on two levels: first, a periodic review of all areas of collaboration between the WCC and the Catholic Church to isolate problems and to suggest directions for the future development of relationships; and second, the promotion of studies on specific themes such as the catholicity and the apostolicity of the church, the common witness and proselytism, the confession of a common faith, and the relationship between the local church and the universal church.[18]

Social commitment represented a second setting of collaboration between the WCC and the Catholic Church. Created in 1968, SODEPAX *(Joint Committee on Society, Development and Peace)* was an office entrusted with the task of promoting greater awareness of the churches' responsibility in the promotion of social justice, economic development, and peace. In the first years of its activity, this body proposed rather prestigious and successful initiatives both in the field of reflection (between 1969 and 1973 conferences were organized on themes such as the theology of development, the means of communication for development and peace, peace and the international community, the role of the church in the development of Asia, and for peace in Northern Ireland) and in the realization of concrete development projects. The success of the initiatives and the elaboration of activities, however, quickly modified the characteristics of this body that became an autonomous agent of action, while both the WCC and the Catholic Church perceived SODEPAX to

---

[18] The reports of the Joint Working Group may be found on the website of the Centro Pro Unione, www.prounione.urbe.it.

be a structure of advisory character. For this reason, beyond the difficulties to retrieve the necessary resources to realize its projects, activity
was progressively reduced until 1980, when this body was dissolved.
SODEPAX was temporarily replaced by a *Joint Consultative Group on
Social Thought and Action* that was to continue its work with more fluid
structures, but in 1988 it also was terminated and its areas of responsibility taken over by the JWG.

The setting of theological reflection also finally saw an intense collaboration between the Catholic Church and the WCC. Since 1968, the
Catholic Church has been a full member of Faith and Order and participates in the activities of the commission with a consistent number
of theologians. In this way, the Catholic tradition has also been able
to contribute directly to the multilateral theological work developed
within the WCC. For example, the presence of the Catholic point of
view is clearly evident in the preparation of the Lima document *Baptism,
Eucharist and Ministry* (1982) that elicited extensive discussion and to
which most churches have made an official response.[19] Currently, Faith
and Order is engaged in an ample study project on the ecclesiological
thematic hinged on the concept of *koinonia*.[20]

With the exception of the full integration of Catholic members in
Faith and Order, all the activities mentioned correspond to the model
of bilateral collaboration among two bodies that maintain their own
autonomy. Establishing relations of this nature between the WCC
and the Catholic Church has seemed to many an anomalous fact or,
at any rate, a provisional and functional solution toward the mutual
knowledge that is necessary in the initial phases of common activity.
Very soon, therefore, the question was raised whether it was possible
and desirable to go beyond the bilateral collaboration to membership
of the Catholic Church in the WCC. The proposal was advanced by

[19] Cf. Commission on Faith and Order, *Baptism, Eucharist and Ministry* (Faith and
Order Paper 111) (Geneva: World Council of Churches, 1982); also published as *Baptism,
Eucharist, Ministry: Report of the Faith and Order Commission, World Council of Churches,
Lima, Peru 1982*, in Harding Meyer and Lukas Vischer, eds., *Growth in Agreement: Reports
and Agreed Statements of Ecumenical Conversations on a World Level* (Ecumenical Documents
II/Faith and Order Paper 108) (New York/Geneva: Paulist Press/World Council of
Churches, 1984) 465–503. The responses of the churches are collected in Max Thurian,
ed., *Churches Respond to Baptism, Eucharist and Ministry: Official Responses to the "Baptism,
Eucharist and Ministry" Text*, Volumes I–VI (Faith and Order Papers 129, 132, 135, 137, 143,
144) (Geneva: World Council of Churches, 1986–1988).

[20] Cf. Commission on Faith and Order, *The Nature and Purpose of the Church: A Stage
on the Way to a Common Statement* (Faith and Order Paper 181) (Geneva: World Council
of Churches, 1998).

Father Roberto Tucci in an intervention to the WCC World Assembly in Uppsala in 1968. In the following year, however, on the occasion of his visit to the ecumenical center in Geneva, while recognizing the progress made in relations between the Catholic Church and the WCC, Paul VI affirmed that the times were not yet ripe for the participation of the Catholic Church in the WCC, and he stressed the necessity of further close examination of the problems posed by such a decision.[21]

Even if from a formal point of view the initiative to request affiliation with the WCC rests exclusively with the Catholic Church, which must make application to this effect to the WCC, the Joint Working Group studied the matter with the aim of offering useful factors to mature the decision, and it synthesized in a document the conclusion of its reflection conducted on possible developments on relations between the Catholic Church and the WCC.[22]

While not impossible in principle, certain difficulties would have to be resolved for a possible membership of the Catholic Church in the WCC. The Catholic Church is a world church, while the member churches of the WCC for the most part are churches with an expanse limited to a determined geographical area. The criteria the WCC uses for acceptance of the churches that ask to enter as members are not, therefore, entirely parallel to the reality of the Catholic Church. Even if for practical reasons it would be desirable to accept as members churches whose size is proportionate to those churches that already belong to the council, the possibility of membership in the WCC of churches of world size cannot be excluded. The JWG document emphasizes that the

[21] Paulus, PP. VI, *The Teachings of Pope Paul VI, 1897–1978* (Città del Vaticano: Libreria editrice vaticana, 1970). "Our increasing cooperation in many fields of common interest sometimes causes a question to surface, namely, should the Catholic Church become a member of the Ecumenical Council? How can we answer this question at this particular time? With fraternal frankness we do not think that the issue of the participation of the Catholic Church is mature to the point where we can give a positive answer. The question still remains hypothetical. It implies grave theological and pastoral problems and therefore it requires close examination, binding us to a great journey that, in all honesty, could be long and difficult" (trans. Luigi Bertocchi, o.s.b.). Paolo VI, *Discorso al Consiglio Ecumenico delle Chiese* [10 giugno 1969] in *Insegnamenti di Paolo VI*, VII (Roma: Tipografia Poliglotta Vaticana, 1970) 397–98.

[22] Cf. Joint Working Group between the Roman Catholic Church and the World Council of Churches, "Patterns of Relationships Between the Roman Catholic Church and the World Council of Churches," *Ecumenical Review* 24:3 (1972) 247–88. The discussion about the possible membership of the Roman Catholic Church in the WCC is reconstructed in detail by J. Grootaers, "An Unfinished Agenda. The Question of Roman Catholic Membership of the World Council of Churches, 1968–1975," *Ecumenical Review* 49:3 (1997) 305–47.

Catholic Church should be represented in a variety of expressions and in its voice on local and universal levels in such a way that participation corresponds with its conviction to be one church and respects local particularities. The solution offered in the document is, therefore, that of a participation as a unique church, but one that at the same time involves patriarchal synods and episcopal conferences.

The measure of representation, then, should be such that, on one hand, it takes into account the variety of components of the Catholic Church, and, on the other hand, it does not make smaller partners disappear as interlocutors in dialogue (from the point of view of numerical consistency, in fact, the members of the Catholic Church are more than double those of member churches of the WCC). After all, at present, representation within the WCC is not determined solely on the basis of proportion with the number of members of churches represented. The document advances the proposal that Catholic representation in world assemblies be not less than one-fifth and not more than one-third of the total number of delegates. The same proportions can also be valid for other structures of the WCC.

The document also calms the fears about the consequences that could derive from the decision to become a member of the WCC: participation in the WCC does not keep the Catholic Church from its exercise of a universal magisterium. Nevertheless, it cannot be denied that, while the Catholic Church practices this way of operating at the universal level, many other churches consider the WCC to be the instrument of such action. They would be able, therefore, to create difficulty in the case of divergences between what is affirmed by the Catholic Church and by the WCC. In this regard, the document affirms that dissent on a decision of the WCC does not necessarily implicate the will of a church to interrupt the dialogue with others. It is, therefore, compatible with a church's continuance in the council. Also, the Catholic understanding of authority and of the role given to the pope should not represent an obstacle, in light of the principle according to which the WCC respects the ecclesiological convictions of its member churches. They would be able, however, to raise problems of a practical nature whose impression would be a relativized authority of the pope.

The proposal of Catholic membership in the WCC had no follow-up. After having affirmed that the Catholic Church can accept the Basis of the WCC, the fourth report of the Joint Working Group (1975) verified that the conditions for entrance did not exist because of a series of difficulties.

To a much greater degree than other churches, the Roman Catholic Church sees its constitution as a universal fellowship with universal mission and structure as an essential element of its identity. Membership could present real pastoral problems to many Roman Catholics because the decision to belong to a world-wide fellowship of churches could easily be misunderstood. Then there is the way in which authority is considered in the Roman Catholic Church and the processes through which it is exercised. There are also practical differences in the mode of operation, including the style and impact of public statements.[23]

The underlying reasons why the Catholic Church did not become a member of the WCC are of different order. But a symptomatic fact can certainly be considered, revelatory of a difficulty—that from the point of view of the Catholic Church remains—to fully enter the dialogue space defined by the structures of the WCC. It must be acknowledged that in principle such participation is not impossible, since also for the Catholic Church the same respect for ecclesiological convictions of which it is bearer would be recognized by all the churches.

Numerous commentators think the fundamental reason that has prevented the Catholic Church from belonging to the WCC is of an ecclesiological nature. Without a doubt, this explanation is shared, but, otherwise from how frequently it is affirmed, the principal obstacle is represented by the analogy of structure more than from the differences existing between the Catholic Church and the WCC. As already mentioned, those belonging to the WCC are ecclesial communities with a limited geographic expanse, corresponding to that of a local church. They spontaneously look upon the WCC as an instrument able to give expression, although still in imperfect form, to the universal communion among the churches. On the contrary, the Catholic Church is convinced that it already realizes this universal communion and has the structures that enable it to manifest and guarantee this communion. Therefore, if the WCC proposes itself to be not only a neutral place of dialogue but a form in which the churches currently live in a certain universal communion, the problem is posed how these institutions can integrate themselves with those rooted in history (for example, the

[23] This report appears as Appendix 6, "The Fourth Official Report of the Joint Working Group between the Roman Catholic Church and the World Council of Churches," in David M. Paton, ed., *Breaking Barriers: Nairobi 1975: The Official Report of the Fifth World Assembly of the World Council of Churches, Nairobi, 23 November–10 December, 1975* (London/Grand Rapids, Mich.: SPCK/Eerdmans Publishing Company, 1976); the quotation is from the section "The Collaboration 1965–1975," 275; it is also on the website of the Centro Pro Unione, www.prounione.urbe.it.

episcopal college and the primacy of the Bishop of Rome) which the Catholic tradition holds necessary for the church.

The WCC assures the ecclesiological convictions of each member church. Still, the Catholic Church more explicitly and consciously seems to believe that possible membership in the WCC would, however, put it in an ecclesially characterized context that involves the acceptance of ecclesial relationships structured in a way different from the communion existing within itself among local churches. On the other hand, these reservations indirectly implicate the recognition of the ecclesial consistence of the WCC and the binding character of the communion that links its member churches. Confirmation of this is found in the fear that WCC assertions would enter into competition with those of the Catholic Church and that the structures of the WCC would be set up as a structure parallel to the magisterium of the Catholic Church on the universal level. This difficulty explains why the Catholic Church has preferred bilateral cooperation with the WCC rather than integration in it.

Bilateral Dialogues

Ecumenical activity of the Catholic Church in the postconciliar period also developed in a second direction to be observed in the beginning of bilateral relationships with the principal ecclesial communions. These relationships can be considered in a certain measure the prolongation and the development of contacts established with observers during Vatican II. Bilateral relationships with different Christian confessions have had different character and function, even if in the period following the council, it is theological dialogue above all that has known the most significant development. In this span of time, bilateral dialogue discloses a form of ecumenical commitment particularly congenial to the Catholic Church which, with its intense activity in this area, has contributed to value confessional federations (Lutheran World Federation, World Alliance of Reformed Churches, World Methodist Council) and the Christian World Communions (Anglican Communion, Orthodox churches) also as agents of ecumenical action. In turn, the confessional federations and the Christian World Communions have established bilateral relationships among themselves.

In the last thirty-five years, a complex network of bilateral dialogues has developed. The Spring 1999 issue of the *Bulletin* of the *Centro Pro Unione* in Rome, which periodically offers an up-to-date bibliography on interconfessional dialogues, reviewed 145 developments at diverse levels, from international to local.[24] It is not possible here to mention all the bilateral dialogues that have developed or are still in progress. We limit ourselves to a representative sampling of the bilateral dialogues developed on the international level in which the Catholic Church has taken part.[25]

A dialogue not well known, but certainly not without importance, has developed between the Catholic Church and the ancient Oriental Orthodox churches (Syriac, Coptic, and Ethiopian). This dialogue has focused on christology and has succeeded to overcome the dissent that brought these churches to refuse the doctrinal formulations of the Councils of Ephesus and Chalcedon. One of the aspects distinguishing this dialogue is that the results of the theological work done enabled the partner churches to take official positions, undersigned by the heads of the churches, in which they declare that the christological controversies that caused a break in ecclesial communion in antiquity have been overcome. Of equal significance, from the theological point of view, is

[24] Cf. *Centro Pro Unione Bulletin* 55 (Spring 1999). [The original bibliography was published as James F. Puglisi and Sever J. Voicu, eds., *A Bibliography of Interchurch and Interconfessional Theological Dialogues* (Rome: Centro Pro Unione, 1984). Annual updates appear in the spring issue of *Centro Pro Unione Bulletin*.] A more complete description of the encounters and themes treated in the principle dialogues is found in the reports of the Faith and Order fora on the dialogues. See Commission on Faith and Order, *The Three Reports of the Forum on Bilateral Conversations (1978–1980)* (Faith and Order Paper 107) (Geneva: World Council of Churches, 1981); Commission on Faith and Order, *Fourth Forum on Bilateral Conversations (1985)* (Faith and Order Paper 125) (Geneva: World Council of Churches, 1985); Commission on Faith and Order, *Fifth Forum on Bilateral Conversations (1990)/International Bilateral Dialogues 1965–1991; List of Commissions, Meetings, Themes and Reports* (Faith and Order Paper 156, compiled by Günther Gaßmann) (Geneva: World Council of Churches, 1991); Commission on Faith and Order, *Sixth Forum on Bilateral Dialogues: Ecumenical Institute Bossey, Switzerland, 8–13 October 1994. Report: International Bilateral Dialogues 1992–1994. List of Commissions, Meetings, Themes and Reports* (Faith and Order Paper 168, compiled by Günther Gaßmann) (Geneva: World Council of Churches, 1995); Commission on Faith and Order, *Seventh Forum on Bilateral Dialogues, 9–14 May 1997, John XXIII Centre, Annecy-le-Vieux, France: Emerging Visions of Visible Unity in the Canberra Statement and the Bilateral Dialogues; Report and Papers Presented. International Bilateral Dialogues 1994–1997; List of Commissions, Meetings, Themes and Reports* (Faith and Order Paper 179, compiled by Alan D. Falconer) (Geneva: World Council of Churches, 1997); Commission on Faith and Order, *Eighth Forum on Bilateral Dialogues* (Faith and Order Paper 190) (Geneva: World Council of Churches, 2002).

[25] The results of the dialogues conducted are documented in Harding Meyer and Lukas Vischer, eds., *Growth in Agreement: Reports and Agreed Statements of Ecumenical Conversations on a World Level* (Ecumenical Documents II/Faith and Order Paper 108) (New York/Geneva: Paulist Press/World Council of Churches, 1984), and in Jeffrey Gros, f.s.c., Harding Meyer and William G. Rusch, eds., *Growth in Agreement II: Reports and Agreed Statements of Ecumenical Conversations on a World Level 1982–1998* (Faith and Order Paper 187) (Grand Rapids, Mich./Geneva: Eerdmans Publishing Company/World Council of Churches, 2000).

the principle applied in these dialogues according to which unity in faith does not necessarily have to be expressed in identical theological formulations but allows for different linguistic expressions.[26]

Since 1980 the Catholic Church has also undertaken a theological dialogue with the Orthodox churches that acknowledge as their head the ecumenical patriarchate of Constantinople. Contacts were actually initiated during Vatican II with the celebrated encounter of Pope Paul VI and Patriarch Athenagoras in Jerusalem in 1964, with a follow-up exchange of visits to Rome and Constantinople and with the lifting of the 1054 excommunications at the end of the council. Characterized by personal contacts that allowed for reestablishing mutual trust and from symbolic gestures expressing the will for reconciliation (dialogue of love), this first phase was followed by a phase of theological examination of controversial issues (dialogue of truth) in 1980. Attention of the Orthodox-Catholic commission concentrated on the themes of church, of sacraments, and of ordained ministry.[27] Following the political changes that took place in eastern Europe, most recent phases of the dialogue have been conditioned by the tensions that have risen between the Orthodox churches and the Eastern Catholic churches. Contemporary pressures, therefore, caused the commission to modify its working agenda and to confront the delicate problem of Uniatism, that is, the position and the significance due the Catholic churches of Eastern Rite on a path whose destination is the reestablishment of communion with the Orthodox churches from which they separated in order to unite themselves to Rome.[28]

[26] Cf., for example, in Erminio Lora, ed., *Enchiridion Vaticanum 4. Documenti Ufficiali della Santa Sede 1971–1973*, the Common Declaration of Paul VI and Mar Ignatius Jacob III (1971), nn. 1113–1116, and the Common Declaration of Pope Paul VI and Shenouda III (1973), nn. 2498–2507; and in Bruno Testacci e Guido Mocellin, edd., *EV 9, Joint declaration of the Pope [John Paul II] and the Syrian Orthodox Patriarch of Antioch [Moran Mar Ignazio Zakka I Iwas]* (1984), nn. 837–46.

[27] Cf. the following statements from the Joint International Roman Catholic-Orthodox Commission for Theological Dialogue: *The Mystery of the Church and of the Eucharist in the Light of the Mystery of the Holy Trinity, Munich, Germany, 30 June–6 July 1982* [Munich Statement], Document 48 in "XXIII. Eastern Orthodox-Roman Catholic Dialogue," in Gros, Meyer, and Rusch, *Growth in Agreement II*, 652–59; *Faith, Sacraments and the Unity of the Church, Bari, Italy, June 1987* [Bari Statement], Document 49 in "XXIII. Eastern Orthodox-Roman Catholic Dialogue," in Gros, Meyer, and Rusch, *Growth in Agreement II*, 660–68; *The Sacrament of Order in the Sacramental Structure of the Church, New Valamo, Finland, 26 June 1988* [New Valamo Statement], Document 51 in "XXII. Eastern Orthodox-Roman Catholic Dialogue," in Gros, Meyer, and Rusch, *Growth in Agreement II*, 671–79.

[28] Cf. *Uniatism: Method of Union of the Past, and the Present Search for Full Communion* [Balamand Statement], Document 52 in "XXIII. Eastern Orthodox-Roman Catholic Dialogue," in Gros, Meyer, and Rusch, *Growth in Agreement II*, 680–85.

Chronologically, dialogues with Eastern churches were preceded by those the Catholic Church held immediately after Vatican II with the churches born from the sixteenth-century Reformation.

After some preliminary contacts (1965–1966), the Lutheran-Roman Catholic international dialogue officially began in 1967 and developed in three successive phases. In the first phase (1967–1971), a recognition of the main issues of the historical controversy between Catholics and Lutherans surrounding the question of the relationship between the Gospel and the church was reached.[29] In the second phase (1973–1984), the topics of the Eucharist and the ministry were treated,[30] and the dialogue sought to delineate a viable way to proceed toward reconciliation between the two churches.[31] In the third phase (1985–1993), the dialogue returned to consider a thematic of general nature and explored the relationship between the doctrine of justification and ecclesiology.[32] In 1995 the dialogue entered its fourth phase, in which it is concerned with the apostolicity of the church.

From 1971 to 1976, the collaboration between Catholics and Lutherans has widened and has also involved World Alliance of Reformed Churches (WARC) in a dialogue on marriage. Since 1970, a bilateral dialogue between the Catholic Church and the World Alliance of Reformed Churches has taken place. This Reformed-Catholic dialogue is less developed than the Lutheran-Roman Catholic dialogue because WARC

---

[29] Cf. *The Gospel and the Church 1972 ("Malta Report")*, in "Lutheran-Roman Catholic Conversations," in Meyer and Vischer, *Growth in Agreement*, 168–89.

[30] Cf. *The Eucharist: Final Report of the Joint Roman Catholic-Lutheran Commission, 1978*, in "Lutheran-Roman Catholic Conversations," in Meyer and Vischer, *Growth in Agreement*, 190–214, and *The Ministry in the Church, 1981*, in "Lutheran-Roman Catholic Conversations," in Meyer and Vischer, *Growth in Agreement*, 248–75.

[31] Cf. *Ways to Community, 1980*, in "Lutheran-Roman Catholic Conversations," in Meyer and Vischer, Growth in Agreement, 215–40. This publication does not include the preface of the document. The document preface is in the original publication, *Ways to Community [1980]* (Geneva; Lutheran World Federation, 1981). Published with *Ways to Community* is the statement issued on the occasion of the 450th anniversary of the *Confessio Augustana*, *All Under One Christ, 1980*, in "Lutheran-Roman Catholic Conversations" in Meyer and Vischer, *Growth in Agreement*, 241–47. Cf. *Facing Unity [: Models, Forms and Phases of Catholic-Lutheran Fellowship], Rome, Italy, 3 March 1984*, Document 42 in "XXI. Lutheran-Roman Catholic Dialogue," in Gros, Meyer, and Rusch, *Growth in Agreement II*, 443–84. Published with *Facing Unity* is the statement issued on the occasion of the 500th anniversary of the birth of Luther, *Martin Luther—Witness to Jesus Christ, Kloster Kirchberg, Germany, 6 May 1983*, Document 41 in "XXI. Lutheran-Roman Catholic Dialogue," in Gros, Meyer, and Rusch, *Growth in Agreement II*, 438–42.

[32] Cf. *Church and Justification [: Understanding the Church in Light of the Doctrine of Justification], Wurzburg, Germany, 11 September 1993*, Document 43 in "XXI. Lutheran-Roman Catholic Dialogue," in Gros, Meyer, and Rusch, *Growth in Agreement II*, 485–565.

has especially encouraged contacts on the local level and on the multi-lateral level among member churches of the WCC.[33] The dialogue has focused on ecclesiology and has by the year 2000 published two documents in which the commission has formulated the elements of consensus and the matters open in respect to the understanding of the church.[34] In 1998 the Reformed-Catholic dialogue took up its third phase.

In the years immediately following Vatican II, the beginning of another important bilateral dialogue took place, that of Anglican-Roman Catholic, that, after a preliminary phase (1967–1968), developed in two successive phases. In the first phase (1970–1981), the Anglican-Roman Catholic International Commission (ARCIC I) treated the topics of Eucharist, ecclesial ministry, and authority in the church.[35] In the second phase (ARCIC II), initiated in 1983, the dialogue examined the question of the relationship between salvation and the church[36] and explored the topic of ethics. Ethics is new ground for ecumenical dialogues. Nevertheless, there are today manifested reasons for dissensions in this area among the churches.[37] In the last period of its work, the commission again took up ecclesiology, furthering the reflection initiated in the first phase on authority in the church and the significance of the Petrine ministry.[38]

In 1967 the Catholic Church began a dialogue with the World Methodist Council that has developed in five successive phases. Controversial

[33] Cf. *The Theology of Marriage and the Problem of Mixed Marriages. Final Report of the Roman Catholic-Lutheran-Reformed Study Commission . . . 1976*, in "Lutheran-Reformed-Roman Catholic Conversations," in Meyer and Vischer, *Growth in Agreement*, 279–306.

[34] Cf. *The Presence of Christ in Church and World: Final Report of the Dialogue between the World Alliance of Reformed Churches and the Secretariat for Promoting Christian Unity, 1977* in "Reformed-Roman Catholic Conversations," in Meyer and Vischer, *Growth in Agreement*, 434–46, and *Reformed-Roman Catholic International Dialogue, Towards a Common Understanding of the Church, Second Phase, 1984–1990*, Document 66 in "XXVII. Reformed-Roman Catholic Dialogue," in Gros, Meyer, and Rusch, *Growth in Agreement II*, 780–818.

[35] Cf. *Final Report 1981* [ARCIC I statements from 1971–1981], in "Anglican-Roman Catholic Conversations," in Meyer and Vischer, *Growth in Agreement*, 62–118.

[36] Cf. *Salvation and the Church, Llandaff, Wales, 3 September 1986*, Document 33 in "XVII. Anglican-Roman Catholic Dialogue," in Gros, Meyer, and Rusch, *Growth in Agreement II*, 315–25, and *Church as Communion, Dublin, Ireland, 6 September 1990*, Document 35 in "XVII. Anglican-Roman Catholic Dialogue," in Gros, Meyer, and Rusch, *Growth in Agreement II*, 328–43.

[37] Cf. *Life in Christ: Morals, Communion and the Church, Venice, Italy, 5 September 1993*, Document 36 in "XVII. Anglican-Roman Catholic Dialogue," in Gros, Meyer, and Rusch, *Growth in Agreement II*, 344–70.

[38] Cf. *The Gift of Authority: Authority in the Church III: An Agreed Statement by the Anglican-Roman Catholic International Commission ARCIC* [Authority III] (London/Toronto/New York: Catholic Truth Society/Anglican Book Centre/Church Publishing Incorporated, 1999).

issues as well as matters related to Christian life and spiritual experience
have been the subjects of common reflection.[39] The year 1972 saw the beginning of a dialogue between the Catholic Church and some representatives of the Pentecostal churches and of the Charismatic movement
present within Protestant and Anglican churches. The themes treated
concern especially the different modalities of the action of the Spirit and
the criteria for its discernment.[40] From 1977, the Catholic Church has
been in dialogue with the Disciples of Christ. This dialogue developed
in two successive phases and concerned themes relative to ecclesiology
and to the theology of the sacraments.[41] In the same year, the Catholic
Church started a dialogue with Evangelical communities on the subject of mission.[42] In 1984 the Catholic Church initiated a dialogue with

---

[39] At the conclusion of each phase of the dialogue a report is published. See *Denver
Report, 1971*, in "Methodist-Roman Catholic Conversations," in Meyer and Vischer, *Growth
in Agreement*, 308–39; *Dublin Report, 1976*, in "Methodist-Roman Catholic Conversations,"
in Meyer and Vischer, *Growth in Agreement*, 340–66; *Honolulu Report, 1981* in "Methodist-
Roman Catholic Conversations," in Meyer and Vischer, *Growth in Agreement*, 367–87;
Towards a Statement on the Church, Fourth Series 1982–1986, Nairobi, Kenya, 1986 [Nairobi
Report], Document 45 in "XXII. Methodist-Roman Catholic Dialogue," in Gros, Meyer,
and Rusch, *Growth in Agreement II*, 583–96,. *The Apostolic Tradition, Fifth Series 1986–1991,
Paris, France, 15 April 1991* [Singapore Report], Document 46 in "XXII. Methodist-Roman
Catholic Dialogue," in Gros, Meyer, and Rusch, *Growth in Agreement II*, 597–617; *The Word
of Life: A Statement on Revelation and Faith, Sixth Series (1991–1996), Baar, Switzerland, 15
November 1995* [Rio de Janeiro Report], Document 47 in "XXII. Methodist-Roman Catholic
Dialogue," in Gros, Meyer, and Rusch, *Growth in Agreement II*, 618–46.

[40] Cf. *Final Report of the Dialogue between the Secretariat for Pontifical Council for Promoting
Christian Unity of the Roman Catholic Church and Leaders of Some Pentecostal Churches and
Participants in the Charismatic Movement within Protestant and Anglican Churches, 1972–1976*,
Document 62 in "XVI. Pentecostal-Roman Catholic Dialogue," in Gros, Meyer, and Rusch,
Growth in Agreement II, 713–20; *Final Report. Dialogue between the Secretariat for Pontifical
Council for Promoting Christian Unity and Some Classical Pentecostals, 1977–1982*, Document
63 in "XVI. Pentecostal-Roman Catholic Dialogue," in Gros, Meyer, and Rusch, *Growth in
Agreement II*, 721–34; *Perspectives on* Koinonia. *Report from the Third Quinquennium of the
Dialogue between the Secretariat for Pontifical Council for Promoting Christian Unity and Some
Classical Pentecostal Churches and Leaders, 1985–1989*, Document 64 in "XVI. Pentecostal-
Roman Catholic Dialogue," in Gros, Meyer, and Rusch, *Growth in Agreement II*, 735–52;
Evangelization, Proselytism and Common Witness, Document 65 in "XVI. Pentecostal-Roman
Catholic Dialogue," in Gros, Meyer, and Rusch, *Growth in Agreement II*, 753–79.

[41] Cf. *Report 1981 [Apostolicity and Catholicity;* Ardfert Text] in "Disciples-Roman
Catholic Conversations" in Meyer and Vischer, *Growth in Agreement*, 153–66; *The Church
as Communion in Christ, St. Louis, Missouri, USA, 7 December 1992*, Document 39 in "XIX.
Disciples of Christ-Roman Catholic Dialogue," in Gros, Meyer, and Rusch, *Growth in
Agreement II*, 386–98.

[42] Cf. *The Evangelical-Roman Catholic Dialogue on Mission, 1977–1984*, Document 40
in "XX. Evangelical-Roman Catholic Dialogue," in Gros, Meyer, and Rusch, *Growth in
Agreement II*, 399–437.

the World Baptist Alliance,[43] and in 1998 it established contacts with the Mennonite World Conference.[44]

This bare listing of dialogues, themes, and documents has a rather sketchy character since it includes only international dialogues in which the Catholic Church participates. In reality, the phenomenon of bilateral dialogue is much more extensive and variegated. Furthermore, it must be remembered that the meaning of the concept of "bilateral dialogue" is not univocal. In fact, the term designates a rather accommodating instrument that, depending upon the task at whose service it is placed, it can assume a totally different character. It suffices to remember that among the bilateral dialogues set up by the Catholic Church, some from the beginning had the aim to create the conditions for ecclesial unity, while others intended only to facilitate better mutual knowledge and respect among communities and to clarify the status of divergences.

Bilateral dialogues have also had a different character under the profile of the ecclesial representation. Especially on the local level, there have been dialogues conducted without any official mandate. They are exclusively under the authority of the participants. Other dialogues have instead had the ratification of their results from ecclesial authorities who have conferred on them a binding character similar to that of official teaching of the churches. Between these two extremes all shades are present, and each dialogue produces a blend each time different from the ecclesial mandate and autonomous responsibility of the participants. In the last decades, the prevailing typology is that of a dialogue carried out by theologians who have an official mandate from their respective churches and that nevertheless develops under their responsibility. In virtue of the official mandate received by members of bilateral commissions, those conducting dialogue can indeed be considered representatives of the churches to which they belong and by which they are trusted. This, however, does not in any case implicate that a normative value of the results of such dialogues is automatically recognized by the churches participating in dialogue. At the end of their work, the commissions bring their findings to their respective churches for evaluation, and, if judged compatible with their own convictions of faith, for approval and reception.

---

[43] Cf. *Summons to Witness to Christ in Today's World: A Report on Conversations, 1984–1988,* Document 38 in "XVIII. Baptist-Roman Catholic Dialogue" in Gros, Meyer, and Rusch, *Growth in Agreement II,* 373–85.

[44] Cf. *Information Service 99* (1998) 219.

The choice of the Catholic Church and other confessional families to privilege bilateral dialogue has not been spared criticism. It has been observed that, instead of helping overcome confessional differences, bilateral dialogue has reinforced them, since each side tends to justify and defend its own position confronting an interlocutor. What is dealt with, then, is a form of ecumenical activity that is not sufficiently binding, that allows the churches to demonstrate sensitivity to ecumenical problems but without openness to change and letting themselves be involved in the journey toward growth in a communion such as that proposed by the WCC. The problem has finally been raised of the coherence of the positions held by churches in dialogue with different partners and of the compatibility of results reached in diverse contexts. In fact, it could happen that, as Lutherans draw closer to Catholics, they would distance themselves from Reformed, with the inevitable consequence of jeopardizing the indivisible character of ecclesial unity.

These criticisms are not totally without foundation, and they point out real risks from which bilateral dialogue must protect itself. Nevertheless, they sometimes seem to emerge from a "monopolistic" frame of mind that attributes exclusive competence for dialogue among the churches to the WCC. In reality, the success of bilateral dialogue seems to depend precisely on its having filled a void. In fact, players have been involved who have remained at the margins of the ecumenical movement and have crossed paths neglected by the direction prevailing within the WCC. For these reasons, bilateral dialogue can be seen as a useful and necessary contribution toward the efforts of reconciliation among the churches.

Before discussing open perspectives regarding the diverse theological themes, bilateral dialogue offered an original contribution to the kind of method to be followed in dealing with the divergences that divide the churches. The first characteristic of this method is *bilaterality*. History shows that the reasons that determined the separations among the churches in various contexts are not the same. It is evident that the polemics between the Latin church and the Byzantine church are not the same as the dissent between the church of Rome and Luther. Since this inheritance of the past conferred an unusual form upon the relations among the confessions, it is natural that ecclesial communities with common historical stories seek to face matters belonging to their own histories in a more direct way. In comparison to the multilateral form, which involves all Christian traditions at the same time, bilateral dialogue appears, therefore, to be the instrument most adapted to confront specifically controversial matters between two Christian confessions, or at any rate, to verify if the reasons that brought division in the past still exist in the same form and justify the permanence of separation. On the other hand, the advantage of the bilateral method weakens when the concentration on particular matters loses sight of the general ecumenical horizon. For this, the most balanced evaluations underline the existing complementarity among the bilateral and multilateral approaches: bilateral dialogues concentrate on issues specifically relevant for the relations between two traditions or churches, while multilateral dialogues "bring all the major Christian traditions into a conversation and provide thereby a framework of common orientations for the bilaterals."[45]

Tied to the bilateral character is also the importance this form of dialogue gives to *history* and the *past.* By this it does not intend to deny an orientation to the future of the ecumenical movement itself, but the destiny of unity cannot be reached if the churches do not make account of their past. This is not only because the identity of ecclesial communities, as that of every social group, derives from long historical processes of the sedimentation of ideas, practices, and institutions, but above all because the process of transmission of the Gospel in time is constitutive of the very reality of the church. Bilateral dialogue holds that comparison cannot be eluded with the ways in which the churches gave witness to the Gospel in the past or that they were held irreconcilable up to the point of exacting mutual condemnation and the rupture of communion. The search for ecclesial unity can be constructed on firm foundations only if based on the reconciliation of memories.

Finally, bilateral dialogue has a markedly *doctrinal* character and has turned its attention to discordant formulations of the faith that have often assumed the form of normative ecclesial teaching and that, up to today, continue to represent an obstacle to communion. Without denying the importance of the challenges the churches are called to face together in today's world, bilateral dialogues have tried in the first place to reach a common formulation of the faith that can constitute the basis for the reestablishment of the ecclesial communion. The principle that has inspired their search is, therefore, the opposite in comparison to what has characterized some currents of the ecumenical movement. If some of the supporters of Life and Work held that "doctrine divides and

[45] Commission on Faith and Order, *Fifth Forum on Bilateral Conversations (1990)/International Bilateral Dialogues 1965–1991; List of Commissions, Meetings, Themes and Reports* (Faith and Order Paper 156, compiled by Günther Gassmann) (Geneva: World Council of Churches, 1991).

service unites," bilateral dialogue grounds itself on the conviction that there is neither ecclesial communion nor the capacity of harmonious action if the churches are not able to formulate together their own faith.

The aspect of bilateral dialogues that has been described briefly shows that they have a goal which at the same time is more modest and more demanding compared with other forms of dialogue. It is a more modest goal because it does not pretend to resolve the ecumenical problem in its totality but is satisfied to contribute a solution to specific matters that are the object of dissent between two ecclesial traditions. At the same time, it is a more demanding goal because it does not surrender to the temptation of disqualifying aprioristically the doctrinal discussions of the past as surpassed and deprived of value, but rather intends to compare them seriously with the truth claims to which doctrines give witness.

Chapter 3

The Structure of Dialogue

The first two chapters introduced the main stages of the journey that brought the churches to encounter one another and to dialogue among themselves in the context of the ecumenical movement. We now want to take up in a more systematic way some matters already considered and offer a more complete and organic description of the phenomenon of ecumenical dialogue, of the conditions that make it possible, of the thematic topics of discussion, and of the pursued goal. With the purpose to better gather the characteristics and structure of dialogue among the churches in ways this has developed in the twentieth century, we hold as useful a preliminary presentation of the methods adopted by the churches during their history to face the dissents that have caused divisions. This allows us to perceive the innovative course of the choice of dialogue as a tool for facing dissent and as a means to promote unity. It also allows us to observe how the will of the churches to remain faithful to their own identity, which has inspired the methods of the past, does not have to be disowned but can find realization in new forms.

Alternatives to Dialogue

In contemporary culture, the recourse to dialogical method as a major way toward the search of truth and toward reaching consensus enjoys general plausibility. On the contrary, authoritarianism and presumption of one party to possess truth entirely and exclusively are stigmatized by public opinion as unacceptable attitudes. This cultural context has also profoundly influenced the methods and the procedure that have been adopted in the churches and among the churches for conflict resolution. If the impact of culture cannot be ignored, neither can the underlying theological reasons for the choice of the comparative method among the churches be underestimated. The case of the Catholic Church shows that objections of a theological nature, which made participation in the ecumenical movement appear incompatible with the Catholic faith, were able to be overcome only thanks to the ecclesiological renewal realized by Vatican II. The challenge here is to understand the reasons that urged the churches to take up the way of ecumenical dialogue and, therefore, to necessarily extricate a complex network of factors, both cultural and theological, without surrendering to suggestions of simple explanations.

We have already mentioned that the recourse to dialogue as a method to establish mutual relationships and to seek solutions to controversies represents a rather recent attainment for most of the churches. A look at the ways the ecclesial relations have been lived in the predialogical period will let us see how the methods followed were modified by time and were gradually surpassed because of the very limits they manifested. To describe the evolution of the methods applied in the comparison of the churches during their separation, the typology proposed by Y. Congar that distinguishes four phases and four different forms of relationship remains valid.[1]

The first form assumed by the comparison of the churches is *polemic controversy,* attested both in the relationships among Eastern and Western Christianity, and in the relationships among the Catholic Church and the churches born out of the Reformation. Polemic represents the first and most spontaneous reaction that takes shape in a context in which the rupture of ecclesial communion is being completed or has just happened. The intent of controversy is to disprove the positions maintained by the opponent and to show the validity of one's own. To such a purpose, point after point of the theses of the counterpart is contested to show the nature of its heresy, its lack of biblical and traditional foundations, and its danger to the faith of Christian people. This way to proceed is clearly recognizable in the controversial theology of the sixteenth century that, in most cases, has assumed as its working base an "index of errors" extracted from the works of the Reformers. In many instances, these lists have also represented the point of departure for the formulation of canons and doctrine by the Council of Trent.

---

[1] Cf. Y. Congar, "Stages of the Ecumenical Dialogue," chapter 1 in *Ecumenism and the Future of the Church* (Chicago: Priory Press, 1967) 15–38.

This way of proceeding, which finds a correspondence in the Protestant field, inevitably leads to atomization of the debate and to its dispersion in a myriad of doctrinal matters. Consequently, it turns out difficult, if not impossible to garner the organic character of the contrasted positions and, still less, to understand the intention of who supports them. From this also derives the difficulty to distinguish what is central from what is secondary, with the result that every difference tends to be considered decisive for authenticity of faith.

In controversial theology, the confutation of the positions of the opponents is strictly tied to the apologetics of its own doctrine and to the defense of the authenticity of the church to which it belongs. A certain "rationalism" also derives from the apologetic conception of the task of theology. In fact, discussion is conducted based on the presumption that religious convictions can be modified on the foundation of rational reasoning. At the same time, it tends to ignore the prominence of psychological, sociological, and historical factors in the constitution of a determined Christian and ecclesial identity. Such a limit is even more evident when it attempts to bring concrete Christian life lived in separate communities to an abstract doctrinal picture. The undeniable defects of the controversy method must not be accentuated to the point of making them assume character traits. In fact, they do not lack examples of polemical confrontation that acutely grasps the heart of the matter. Altogether, this method nevertheless already reveals itself as unsuitable to the understanding of the effective terms of dissent and even more the real identity of separate communities. Obviously then, reconciliation among the churches does not constitute an objective reasonably pursuable by following this way.

If polemics is the spontaneous reaction that accompanies the rise of dissent, the passing of time, beyond increasing the mutual extraneousness, also attenuates the sourness of opposition and leaves place for *irenic controversy*. The term suggests that the intent of confutation of the opponent remains, but criticism is conducted in a more serene spirit, "pacific," and inspired by a more sincere effort of understanding. In the development of relationships among the churches in the West, this new attitude finds expression in the work of the French bishop Jacques Bénigne Bossuet (1627–1704), *An Exposition of the Doctrine of the Catholic Church in Matters of Controversie* (1671). The author observes that the reason why Protestants turned against the Catholic Church in many cases was not the dissent on dogma or on the central contents of faith but a series of historical superstructures and theological speculations, as, for example, those elaborated by Scholastic reflection. The contribution of Bossuet is important from the methodological point of view because it underlines the necessity to distinguish between what is essential— and, therefore, it characterizes the identity of a church in an irreducible way—and the secondary elements, between official teaching and the simple theological opinion. Accompanying this is the attempt to reach a more organic understanding of the positions sustained from other churches. This does not mean that Bossuet had been the promoter of an ecumenism *ante litteram*. His perspective remains clearly controversial, as his *The History of the Variations of the Protestant Churches* (1688) shows beyond any shade of doubt. In this work the author intends to demonstrate the falsehood of the position of the "religion claimed reformed" and the principal argument to bear this thesis represented exactly by the "variations" known from Protestant doctrine that documents the inauthenticity of the faith of the churches of the Reformation. This will become a model rather diffused in the Catholic interpretation of the Reformation, and it will contribute to accredit a reading that insists on the variations respecting the most ancient tradition of the faith and the divisions that were multiplied among the churches of the Reformation.

The eighteenth century affirms a new approach to the differences among Christian confessions known as *symbolic comparative*. The name derives from symbolic writings, that is, from the official confessions of faith of the different churches (the term refers above all to the documents of the sixteenth-century Reformation) that become the point of privileged reference for the exposition of doctrines. The most important Catholic exponent of this position is Johann Adam Möhler (1796–1838) with his *Symbolik oder Darstellung der dogmatischen Gegensätze der Katholiken und Protestanten nach ihren öffentlichen Bekenntnisschriften* (Mainz, 1832).[2] The work matures within the German academic environment, in which Protestant theological faculties had introduced courses that intended to offer students an organic exposure to the existing doctrinal differences among confessions. Möhler proposes this use in the Catholic setting because:

> Certainly those, who are called to take the lead in theological learning, may be justly expected to acquire a solid and comprehensive knowledge of the tenets of the religious communities, that for so long a time have

[2] Cf. J. A. Möhler, *Symbolism: Exposition of the Doctrinal Differences between Catholics and Protestants as Evidenced by Their Symbolical Writings* (New York: Crossroad Publishing Company / A Crossroad Herder Book, 1997).

stood opposed to each other in mutual rivalry, and still endeavour to maintain this their position. Justly are they required not to rest satisfied by any means with mere general, uncertain, obscure, vague, and unconnected notions upon the great vital question, which Holy Spirit not only for three hundred years, continually agitated the religious life of Europe, but has in part so deeply and mightily convulsed it.[3]

The most significant innovation, however, concerns the method used in the exposition and the scientific criteria from which it is inspired. The symbolic can be defined as "the scientific exposition of the doctrinal differences among the various religious parties opposed to each other, in consequence of the ecclesiastical revolution of the sixteenth century, as these doctrinal differences are evidenced by the public confessions or symbolic books of those parties."[4] This implicates abandonment of the primarily polemic and apologetic finality in order to truly seek exact understanding of the terms of dissent. On the other hand, Möhler is also aware that it is not possible to realize this program situated from a neutral point of view, and he openly declares to assume the Catholic point of view. This, nevertheless, does not eliminate the scientific character of the reconstruction of confessional positions, as the personal point of view does not annul the reliability of the work done by the historian. The assumption of a point of view is rather necessary precisely in order to appropriate the studied object.

> A bare narrative of facts, even when accompanied with the most impartial and solid historical research, will not suffice; nay, the individual proportions of a system of doctrine must be set forth, in their mutual concatenation and their organic connection. Here, it will be necessary to decompose a dogma into the elements out of which it has been formed, and to reduce it to the ultimate principles whereby its author had been determined; there, it will be expedient to trace the manifold changes which have occurred in the dogma: but at all times must the parts of the system be viewed in their relation to the whole, and be referred to the fundamental and all-pervading idea (*Grundidee*).[5]

For Möhler, then, any effort to understand the confessions must lead to gathering the last root of doctrinal differences and, finally, the same essence of the confessions. The polemical moment here is surpassed in favor of an approach that aims at a scientific understanding

[3] Ibid., xxiii.
[4] Ibid., 1.
[5] Ibid., 1–2.

of the positions and at isolating the original idea from which a religious system draws its unity. The privileged reference to official confessions, then, allows for not attributing to an ecclesial community positions held only by some theologians. The limit of this approach derives from its exclusive concentration on the doctrinal dimension, while ecclesial life also takes shape and assumes its own character in other contexts such as liturgy, spirituality, and praxis.

The fourth model of relationship among the churches is represented by *ecumenical dialogue,* the historical development of which was illustrated in the preceding chapters and the structure of which will now be studied in a more precise way. Before examining this, it may be useful to recall the characteristic elements of the methods used in the past to verify what has been surpassed and what, notwithstanding appearances, still remains in the ecumenical phase in which the churches have entered.

The historical evolution of the shape of relations among the churches shows how the matter of *truth* has always had a central importance. Even if in forms that no longer correspond to actual sensibility, the churches have affirmed that their existence depends on the recognition of the truth of the Gospel, and that this truth constitutes the fundamental criterion of the unity they are called to realize in history. Personal contrasts, unmentionable reasons, party interests, and finally, sin weigh heavily in determining the rise of dissent and division, but they cannot obscure an equally important datum: the truth of the confession of faith has been fought for. From this point of view, "controversy," however called and whatever the shapes in which it finds expression, remains an element of theological discourse that cannot be eliminated. It is in fact born of a characteristic belonging to Christian language; that is, from the inseparable bond between its capacity to positively state the truth of the Gospel while discerning truth from error, therefore distancing itself from expressions or ways of acting incompatible with Christian truth and that compromise ecclesial communion. Such a demand cannot be revoked by any ecumenical etiquette or by a spirit of tolerance imposed by culture.[6]

---

[6] It is interesting to observe how the concepts of "heresy" and "excommunication," judged by many a residue of the past and even embarrassing for the Catholic Church that also exercises a magisterium with binding authority, have in our day been rediscovered in the context of the struggle let loose within the German Protestant church *(Kirchenkampf)* following the support part of it has given to Nazi ideology; on the position of D. Bonhoeffer comparing A. Gallas, *Ánthropos téleios. L'ittinerario di Bonhoeffer nel conflitto tra cristianesimo e modernità* (Brescia: Queriniana, 1995) 257–62. Analogous themes are also found in the

Once it is established that the matter of truth cannot be excluded from the consideration of the relations among the churches, it remains necessary to specify what is the most correct way to intend the truth of the Gospel and the relationship with it of individual believers and Christian communities that welcome and witness to it. From this point of view, the model of controversy appears problematic first of all because it is based on an inadequate understanding of truth received from revelation. In fact, in the various forms it has assumed in the course of history, controversy has generally understood revelation as a set of propositions whose truth is guaranteed by the authority of the God who reveals and has reduced faith to the recognition of the truth of such propositions. The nature of the method of controversy, therefore, derives not only—and not even primarily—from the fact that it does not correspond more to the spirit of tolerance diffused in culture, but first of all from a reductive way to conceive revelation and faith comprised of exclusively doctrinal and objective terms.

Overcoming "predialogical" methods in the comparison of the churches has kept pace with the effort achieved by theology to understand revelation and faith in a more adequate way. Such development has determined the progressive introduction of corrections on numerous points. On the "objective" side, the organic and unitary character of Christian truth is perceived, which is not reducible to a list of propositions but that coincides with the person and the historical event of Jesus. From this derives a diverse understanding of doctrine proposed by the church which, if, on one hand, certainly states the content of revelation and renders it accessible, on the other hand, it cannot be immediately identified with revelation nor constitute as such the ultimate end of faith. In fact, according to the famous motto of Thomas of Aquinas, the act of faith does not have as its end the concept of which doctrine is served but the same reality of God with which the believer establishes personal communion.[7] On the side of the believing individual ["subject"], the proper character of the act of faith is gathered in a clearer way that is not comparable to the conclusion of a syllogism but is realized as an undeducible act of freedom within concrete historical conditions.

---

theology of K. Barth, and they explain his distance from the ecumenical movement during the 1930s; cf. T. Herwig, *Karl Barth und die Ökumenische Bewegung. Das Gespräch zwischen Karl Barth und Willem Adolf Visser 't Hooft auf der Grundlage ihres Briefwechsels 1930–1968* (Neukirchen: Neukirchener Verlag, 1998) 24–25.

[7] "Actus autem credentis non terminatur ad enuntiabile, sed ad rem," (*ST* II–II q. 1, a. 2, ad 2). Cf. L. Sartori, *San Tommaso d'Aquino e la fede ecumenica,* in *Teologia ecumenica. Saggi* (Padova: Gregoriana, 1987) 283–95.

From this point of view, the reflection of Y. Congar is exemplary. Resorting entirely to traditional categories in Catholic theology, it came to affirm in 1937 the necessity to revise the judgment formulated on the condition of Christians belonging to other churches. They are incorporated into the church by means of baptism, and, although they grow in a context that is objectively lacking the fullness of faith and of the means of salvation of which the church has been equipped, can live an authentic Christian and ecclesial life since theirs is a condition of invincible ignorance. In the case of a "dissident" who finds himself in

> such conditions that adherence, objectively astray, nevertheless leads straight to Christ and to true membership of His Church. He has the faith of Christ and truly belongs to His Church even though he has not the true faith and does not exteriorly belong to the true Church. He worships God truly, even if he does not worship Him in truth. . . .[8]

This Christian cannot be called heretical, because present in him is only the material element of heresy, not the formal element, that is, the stubbornness to sustain it.

Finally, it must be remembered how the sense of history and historicity reveals itself as a determining factor in diminishing plausibility to the predialogue methods and has in general stimulated a revision of the way to conceive revelation and faith. When revelation is conceived as a historical event, theology must explain how access to it is possible through witnesses. The canonical Scriptures, also guaranteed by the Spirit as a reliable witness, remain a human and historical word, and because of this insist on being interpreted. Interpretation, then, is never a neutral operation but is influenced by the context in which it happens, by the issues posed by the interpreters, and by the methods to which they resort. Just the same, the process of translating the revealed message into a different language and cultural horizon demands the assumption of categories that, on one hand, allow a more comprehensible formulation, but on the other hand, are also limited and implicate the acceptance of a perspective that is inevitably partial. Every formulation of faith, therefore, has a perspective character and cannot expect to exhaust the truth of revelation. In relation to the ecumenical problem, a clearer perception of the historicity of the contrasted formulations of faith has, therefore, contributed to perceive them in their non-

[8] Y. Congar, *Divided Christendom: A Catholic Study of the Problem of Reunion* (London: Geoffrey Bles, 1939) 232; cf. ibid., 224–48.

"absolute" character and to place them within the context from which it is possible to draw out the intention that inspires them.

The combination of the integrity of these elements, united with the experience of personal encounter among believers of different confessions, has opened the way to dialogue. Unlike controversy—polemic or irenic—dialogue recognizes that the separated churches and the believers who form them cannot adequately be understood limiting themselves to using categories of truth and error. The witness of the faith of other churches must first all be listened to and understood in its self-presentation and in the intentions it manifests. On the other hand, the search for understanding does not only have the purpose to reach the most possible accurate description of the confessional positions. It must also intend to create the conditions for reconciliation among the churches. To this end, after having recognized the legitimacy of the interlocutors with whom one enters into relationship as individuals capable of dialogue, what must inevitably be posed is the matter of the truth of the confession of faith upon which is founded ecclesial communion.

Dialogue and Ecumenical Dialogue

The distance realized and the attention reserved for the development of the ecumenical movement must not let it be forgotten that, before being an ecclesial fact, dialogue is a universal human phenomenon. It has its root in the social nature of the human person and is but an aspect of the vast and complex phenomenon of *communication*. Dialogue can be defined as: "a reciprocal process of communication between a sender and a receiver (dialogue partner) about an object of common interest; this process takes place in a given situation through the medium of language."[9] If it is analyzed in a more detailed manner, the phenomenon of dialogue garners the presence of the following constitutive elements that determine its structure.

1. Because there is dialogue, it is necessary that there are at least two *interlocutors*, personal subjects of the communication.
2. They must have something to say, a *message* to communicate.

---

[9] W. Beinert, "Der ökumenische Dialog als Einübung in die Klärung theologischer Differenzen," in Hans Jörg Urban und Harald Wagner, Hrsg., *Handbuch der Ökumenik* (Im Auftrag des J.-A.-Möhler-Instituts). Bände III/1 (Paderborn: Verlag Bonifatius-Druckerei, 1987) 80–81.

3. The communication among the interlocutors has as its goal to arouse *consensus,* and this happens when the receiver recognizes the *truth* of the message that has been communicated to him.
4. Consensus makes possible a *communion* among the interlocutors which, through dialogue, they reach the awareness to share determined knowledge, determined convictions, values; this makes possible a *common action* that implicates the presence of objectives and presuppositions shared in a more explicit and conscious way.
5. Consensus that allows a common action is not only the result of the dialogue, but it is also its *presupposition;* in fact, it would be impossible to dialogue if there was not a common base on which the interlocutors can encounter one another. Common language is the most evident expression of this preexisting consensus to dialogue.

This structure can be verified in all social groups. In them are developed communication processes that render possible a common life and action, creating consensus on shared values and goals. At the same time, every social group exists only because it presupposes a previous consensus, produced by members of the group, but which has the tendency to institutionalize itself and, therefore, to assume an independent existence regarding the will of those who have produced it. The constitution of a state represents an exemplary case of consensus produced and presupposed at the same time: its norms are established through a formation process of the consensus, but once fixed and in absence of modifications, they become the fundamental proposal of living together, even for successive generations that have not contributed to producing such consensus.

The concept of dialogue has also been fruitful from the theological point of view. It in fact lends to describing the relationship between revelation and faith, between the word God addresses to humankind and the human response evoked from that very word. Vatican II assumes this perspective when in the constitution *Dei Verbum* it describes the event of revelation as a historical dialogue which God interweaves with God's people: "By thus revealing himself God, who is invisible (see Col 1, 15; 1 Tm 1,17), in his great love speaks to humankind as friends (see Ex 33, 11; Jn 15, 14-15) and enters into their life (see Bar 3, 38), so as to invite and receive them into relationship with himself" (*DV* 2). The image of dialogue that tends to personal communion allows for overcoming a reductive vision of revelation, understood as communication of truth inaccessible to human reason, and for considering it in its character of historical event oriented to the salvation of humanity. In terms even more explicit, the theme is found in the encyclical of Paul VI, *Ecclesiam Suam* (1964) where the "dialogue of salvation *(colloquium salutis)*" is identified as the first source from which rushes each dialogue the church establishes in the realization of its mission.

> Revelation, too, that supernatural link which God has established with man, can likewise be looked upon as a dialogue. In the Incarnation and in the Gospel it is God's Word that speaks to us. . . . Indeed, the whole history of man's salvation is one long, varied dialogue, which marvelously begins with God and which He prolongs with men in so many different ways.[10]

An appeal turned to human freedom, revelation in the moment in which it is welcomed in history creates a community that witnesses to the Word of God and professes its faith. The church, therefore, too, can be thought of as a structured dialogical reality, not only because it is formed by believers who respond with faith to the Word of God (vertical dimension), but also because it is in the church that the proclamation of the Gospel takes place, to which the confession of faith (horizontal dimension) responds. The vertical dimension of dialogue that weaves between God and humans, and the horizontal dimension of dialogue, constituted by the proclamation of the Word and by the confession of faith, are not then two proportionally distinct and separable realities. In fact, it is in the horizontal process of communication among human persons and not elsewhere that the encounter with the Word of God takes place, that faith is born, and that the possibility to access communion with God is opened.

The interpenetration and the inseparable bond between the two dimensions mentioned constitute the central nucleus of the mystery of the church: *communion* understood as transcendent reality that comes from on high and renders itself historically perceivable, creates the processes of communication that constitute the church as the place where communion with God and among believers is lived. S. Dianich rightly indicates in the "communion that is born from proclamation" the event that stands at the origin of the church and defines its profound nature.[11] For the New Testament, in fact, the beginning of the church is connected to the proclamation of the Gospel which, received in faith, creates a bond of communion between the apostolic witness and the recipients of its

---

[10] *Ecclesiam Suam* 70.
[11] Cf. S. Dianich, *La chiesa mistero di comunione* (Torino: Marietti, 1977²) 56–69.

preaching. This event does not only represent the *beginning* of the church in a chronological sense, but in it theological reflection can recognize the *principio* that explains the reality of the church as such.[12] In fact, beyond establishing itself from a network of communication among those who have received the Gospel and become believers, also found in the communion born of proclamation is the constitutive reference to the event of Jesus that forms the normative and irreplaceable content of the message, and to the communion of believers in the Spirit with the risen Lord and through him with the Father.

This ecclesiological vision does nothing beyond recapturing in a systematic form the elements recorded in the prologue of the First Letter of John:

> We declare to you what was from the beginning, what we have heard, what we have seen with our eyes, what we have looked at and touched with our hands, concerning the word of life—this life was revealed, and we have seen it and testify to it, and declare to you the eternal life that was with the Father and was revealed to us—we declare to you what we have seen and heard so that you also may have fellowship with us; and truly our fellowship is with Father and with his Son Jesus Christ (1 John 1:1-3).

The apostolic witness connects therefore with the story of Jesus—the coming of the Word in the flesh—and as a whole creates a communion that does not limit itself to the horizontal dimension but is communion with the Father and with the Son.

The church is constituted by these processes of communication that create a communion not episodic but endowed with a stability in time and such to be shaped by the Christian community as a recognizable entity within history. The communion born of proclamation is extended therefore in the process of *tradition (paradosis)* that comprises the totality of ways in which the church transmits the Gospel and actualizes the original event of salvation:

> "what has been handed down from the apostles" includes everything that helps the people of God to live a holy life and to grow in faith. In this way the church, in its teaching, life and worship, perpetuates and hands on to every generation all that it is and all that it believes (*DV* 8).

Understood in this way, tradition is not depleted in its doctrinal moment. It also embraces the sacraments and the entire worship of the

---

[12] Cf. S. Dianich, *Ecclesiologia. Questioni di metodo e una proposta* (Cinisello Balsamo [MI]: Paoline, 1993) 94–108.

church, the form of community life, and Christian conduct in the world. What is dealt with in the final analysis is the communion that continues to be realized in time and maintains a substantial homogeneity with its beginning. It thus assures the permanence of the church's identity.

The existing nexus between ecclesial communion and the communicative processes the church activates in the realization of its mission lends to understanding why contemporary ecclesiology has retrieved some terms formulated by the philosophy of language and communication theory in order to illustrate the nature of the church.[13] Beyond legitimizing, such an assumption is useful to show that the church grafts itself to the structures of human sociality and realizes them in original form, on condition, however, to introduce some corrections in the conceptual instrument borrowed from the philosophical analysis of communication. Two aspects are decisive from this point of view. In the first place, theology has to think out a process of communication that does not resolve itself in its horizontal dimension but that integrates the vertical component. It is God in this act of self-revelation that puts into motion the communicative process constitutive of the church, and this transcendent dimension must be recognizable in the human communicative processes, confined to a separate supernatural level. In the second place, the phenomenon of communication does not exhaust itself in the language that would constitute the reality *simpliciter*. The communicative process represented by ecclesial tradition does not only intend to say something about the extralinguistic reality in general. It also makes an essential reference to the historical event of Jesus, accessible through apostolic witness. Within the communicative processes that constitute the church, therefore, not all issues are equal. The apostolic norm—attested in a manner originating from Scripture and actualized in the diverse forms of ecclesial witness—constitutes the normative and irreplaceable content upon which every ecclesial communicative process must be measured.

This structure could be verified in many aspects of ecclesial life. We turn in particular to the area of the confession of faith due to its importance for ecumenical relations.

[13] An example of this assumption is found in M. Kehl, *La Chiesa. Trattato sistematico di ecclesiologia cattolica* (Cinisello Balsamo [MI] San Paolo, 1995) 131–50. On the positions of contemporary ecclesiology in connection with this and the problems raised therein, cf. S. Dianich, "Teorie della comunicazione ed ecclesiologia," in D. Valentini, ed., *L'ecclesiologia contemporanea* (Padova: Messaggero, 1994) 134–78.

The confession of faith is the faithful response to the Word of God that finds a public expression and a formulation in which the members of the Christian community are recognized unanimously. The original context in which it is born is that of the worship where it represents the full expression of gratitude in the reception of the gift of salvation and the truth the Word of God discloses. Precisely because it manifests the reception of the Word of God, the confession of faith often assumes the form of repetition and confirmation of the message proclaimed. Also recognized in this expressive formula are the roots of the "doctrinal" function of the confession of faith which, as a response to the Word of God, it synthetically repeats and reaffirms as the content of truth. The confession of faith, therefore, is originally the expression of praise and gratitude (doxology), but not without content. On the contrary, it has a content that corresponds to the truth of the Word received in faith.

Precisely in virtue of its ability to speak the truth of the Gospel, the confession of faith also functions as a criterion for ecclesial communion. In fact, it can be used as a yardstick to establish concretely if an individual believer or the Christian community as a whole receives the Gospel message in a real and integral way or if they distance themselves from it. The criterion of right faith, therefore, also establishes the borders of ecclesial belonging. In the early church, these processes can be gathered with particular evidence. The baptismal symbol, born in the liturgical context, has represented the base upon which the councils have progressively introduced dogmatic clarifications made necessary from the rise of controversies. In such situations, it is not that dialogue has been the path taken in order to reach formulation of the common faith. The councils, in fact, can be thought of as a dialogical process through which the church seeks to reestablish the harmony of the confession of faith that constitutes the base of its unity. The result of such a process—the symbol of faith and other dogmatic formulas—on one hand intends to be a faithful expression of apostolic witness, and on the other hand, it assumes the function of criterion of ecclesial communion. For exactly this reason with the same action, with which it says that consensus in the confession of faith is the foundation of ecclesial communion, it also traces a line of demarcation in the confrontation of those who do not accept this consensus.

The conciliar practice of the early church offers a model of a methodology that, through the search for consensus, has the purpose to reach a new binding formulation of the faith. The subsequent councils and synods of antiquity and of the epochs show in fact that, when dissent regarding the confession of faith or church discipline is manifested, recourse is made to dialogue between the authorized representatives of the local churches to strengthen the foundation of ecclesial communion. The need of such a binding formulation is noted in a particularly acute way when the previously existing consensus gets lost, and its "reconstruction" is made necessary. At the base of the search of a common formulation of faith is the conviction that Eucharist cannot be celebrated together and ecclesial life in its multiple expressions cannot be shared if it is not possible to formulate common faith. The dialogical process put in action sees, then, the interaction of the following elements: the biblical witness; the symbols of faith and the normative early texts; the ministry of pastors; the reflection of theologians; and the sense of faith of the entire people of God.

Dialogue is, therefore, perceived in a particularly clear form as constitutive of ecclesial life itself when dissent rises up that puts communication within the church in crisis and threatens the presuppositions of common life. In such situations a decision must be reached through confrontation among the different positions. The result of common reflection, however, does not only have its own authority that derives from matters that sustain it and, much less, is it reducible to relationships of force that determine the prevalence of one part over another. It corresponds to the conscience of faith of the church that, in the very act with which it affirms its obedience to the Word of God, it also pronounces authoritative judgment on how much it corresponds to the truth of the revealed message.

The dialogical process put into effect to reconstruct communion in the confession of the one faith has not always been successful. Church history shows that the councils have often had as consequence the rise or the deepening of fractures with determined local churches or Christian groups. All separations are caused by the failure of dialogue and represent the effect of the incapacity of the parties in conflict to renew concord in the confession of faith. Each side, in fact, holds that fidelity to the Gospel imposes denying communion to one who dissents on decisive matters for the integrity of the Christian faith.

The dialogue the ecumenical movement has fostered to renew among the churches has as its primary scope to again make possible the common confession of faith and to create in this way the conditions for the reestablishment of ecclesial communion. In many aspects it represents the resumption of the "conciliar" method that has a constant presence in the history of the church. It cannot, however, be denied that a difference exists between conciliar praxis understood in the strict sense and the paths traversed by the ecumenical movement. Dialogue carried out in councils and in synods intends to strengthen threatened unity that nevertheless still exists since the dissents do not prevent the common celebration of the Eucharist. In the case of ecumenical dialogue, the objective of the encounter is to reconstruct unity in the confession of faith among communities that have broken communion for some time. The context in which ecumenical dialogue develops, therefore, can be characterized as a "preconciliar" situation and the goal it pursues is to create the conditions so that the churches can celebrate a council together.

At the end of this section we can retrieve the scheme used for describing dialogue as a universal human phenomenon and to point out specific contents that ecumenical dialogue as such assumes.

1. The subject of dialogue is the *churches and ecclesial communities.*
2. The goal of dialogue is to find a *consensus* that makes possible a common *confession of faith.*
3. The confession of faith cannot have any content except that of the *apostolic faith* upon which the church is founded and from the fidelity to which its integrity depends. Ecumenical dialogue is completely misunderstood if it is reduced to the search for a compromise that places matters of faith in parenthesis.
4. Common confession of faith makes possible *a common ecclesial life* that embraces all milieus: confession of faith, celebration of sacraments, exercise of ministry, and witness in the world.
5. A consensus also exists that *precedes* the beginning of dialogue and is constituted by the common patrimony of faith that remains despite historical divisions, and that represents the base upon which it is possible to establish relationships.

The considerations presented intend to suggest that the decision to take up the journey of dialogue in the search of reconciliation among the churches does not represent a neutral option, motivated simply by the effectiveness demonstrated by this method or from its plausibility in the context of contemporary culture. The choice of dialogue corresponds to the nature of the church. Since it is constituted by a communicative process realized through witness to the Gospel and confession of faith, dialogue represents the path to take when concord in the confession of faith diminishes and, as a consequence, ecclesial communion is broken among believers in Christ.

In the Search of a Common Expression of the Apostolic Faith

One who examines the themes treated by ecumenical dialogue and by the texts produced by them draws the impression of finding oneself in an inextricable forest. The extreme variety of themes is in fact hardly referable to unity. Nevertheless, beyond the first impression, a point of view exists that unifies and gives coherence to the myriad of thematic particulars subject to discussion in the commissions: the scope pursued by the major part of ecumenical dialogues is the search of a common formulation of the apostolic faith. The discernment the subject of dialogue is to work toward this goal found a happy formulation in the letter in which the Commission on Faith and Order asked the churches to express in an official way their own judgment of the extent to which the Lima document (1982) is able to be affirmed regarding baptism, Eucharist, and ministry. The churches were asked "the extent to which your church can recognize in this text the faith of the Church through the ages."[14] The formulation of the question contains an invitation to go beyond the simple verification of the correspondence of the doctrine expressed in the text. It is an invitation to examine the positions of the different confessions or the letter of biblical witness. It indicates as criterion in the evaluation of the text a formulation of the faith that the churches have lived and transmitted through centuries and that does not immediately coincide with any particular confessional position. In this way, it suggests that the primary purpose of ecumenical dialogue is to help the churches find anew their unity, creating the condition for the mutual recognition of the faith transmitted by the apostles and preserved in a plurality of traditions.[15]

This search does not start at zero. Ecumenical dialogue is possible only because a common patrimony of faith has remained intact despite divisions. For this reason, an encounter is possible among interlocutors who have not lost the basic vocabulary and foundational grammar of the Christian language and, therefore, not having become total strangers, can mutually understand each other and truly enter into dialogue. The doctrinal basis of the World Council of Churches is related to this presupposition of dialogue. This basis not only is the foundation of the

[14] *Baptism, Eucharist, Ministry: Report of the Faith and Order Commission, World Council of Churches, Lima, Peru, 1982,* in Meyer and Vischer, *Growth in Agreement,* Preface, 469.

[15] Realistically, therefore, one must admit that every community sees this "faith of the churches throughout the centuries" through the filter of its own confessional position because each deems to have transmitted faithfully the apostolic heritage.

churches' being together, indicated in trinitarian faith, but also the condition that makes possible the dialogue in which they have decided to commit themselves. A similar formulation is also made by Vatican II when it enumerates the elements Catholics have in common with other churches with which they intend to enter into dialogue. The section of the Decree on Ecumenism dedicated to Western churches and ecclesial communities speaks of "those Christians who openly confess Jesus Christ as God and Lord and as the one mediator between God and human beings, to the glory of the one God, Father, Son and holy Spirit" (*UR* 20). Conciliar affirmation is not equal to the simple acceptance of the position that there is not dissent on this doctrinal point. It can be read as an indication of the center and of the foundation of Christian faith from which it had to depart in order to seek consensus also on controversial matters.

All of this has evident consequences to follow on the level of method. Ecumenical dialogue cannot limit itself to making a list of matters on which there is consensus and of questions on which there is dissent, in the hope that on the latter a resolve can be found. Beginning with common faith, it must discern a criterion that judges the different positions, a dynamic factor that puts them in motion and makes them converge. The preciseness of the methodology of ecumenical dialogue received conclusive momentum on the occasion of the Third World Conference on Faith and Order held in Lund (Sweden) in 1952. At Lund, reflection took initiatives from the examination of the limits of the comparative method that dominated ecumenical discussion up to this time. Necessary in the initial phases of dialogue for interlocutors to get to know one another, comparison of different conceptions of the church had reached a dead end. In fact, such a way of proceeding not only revealed itself ineffective in the promotion of unity, it paradoxically also risked strengthening an apologetic attitude in the interlocutors, and, therefore, deepening existing divisions. To relaunch the dialogue, it was necessary to find a new point of departure. And it is exactly this methodological principle that begins to define itself in the message addressed to the churches by the conference participants.

> We have seen clearly that we can make no real advance toward unity if we only compare our several conceptions of the nature of the Church and the traditions in which they are embodied. But once again it has been proved true that as we seek to draw closer to Christ we come closer to one another. We need, therefore, to penetrate behind our divisions to a deeper and richer understanding of the mystery of the God-given union

of Christ with His Church. We need increasingly to realize that the separate histories of our Churches find their full meaning only if seen in the
perspective of God's dealings with His *whole* people.[16]

It was evident that an immediate solution, almost miraculous, of
all controversial issues could not be expected from the recognition of
the centrality of Christ as criterion for dialogue among the churches.
Application of the suggested criterion to particular issues is, in fact, all
but deprived of difficulty. Nevertheless, what was elaborated at Lund
represents a methodological indication that cannot be underestimated
because it suggests the necessity of a criterion that is superior and able
to overcome the absolutization of contrasted confessional positions.

The principle of the *hierarchy of truths* in the Decree on Ecumenism
of Vatican II is oriented along the same lines: "When comparing doctrines with one 'hierarchy' of truths [Catholic theologians] recall that an
order or 'hierarchy' of the truths of Catholic doctrine exists, varying in
their connection with the foundation of the Christian faith" (*UR* 11).[17] In
light of the teaching of Vatican II, this "foundation of the Christian faith"
can be identified with Christ as the center of Christian revelation.

The principles of christological concentration and of the hierarchy of
truths ought not function, however, in a reductive sense. The search for
a "least common denominator" among the doctrines of the confessions
represents an inadequate path because it ignores the organic character
of the content of Christian revelation, and it reverts in a quantitative
conception of propositions of the truth of faith. It is necessary instead to
depart from the center in order to reach a consensus that extends to the
foundational articulations of Christian faith. A model of articulations of
the essential contents of the faith is offered by the symbols of faith of the
early church, accepted by most Christian churches, even if with different interpretations. From this point of view, the results merit attention:
from the study promoted by Faith and Order that explored the possibility of a common explanation of the faith formulated in the symbols of
the early church.[18] In particular, the Nicene-Constantinopolitan Symbol

[16] Lukas Vischer, "Lund, Third World Conference on Faith and Order, August 15–28,
1952," chapter 4 in *A Documentary History of the Faith and Order Movement 1927–1963* (St.
Louis: Bethany, 1963) n. 2, pp. 85–86.

[17] On the theological precedents of the formula and on the concept of revelation implied cf. W. Henn, *The Hierarchy of Truths according to Yves Congar, O.P.* (Roma: Pontificia
Università Gregoriana, 1987).

[18] Cf. *Confessing the One Faith: An Ecumenical Explication of the Apostolic Faith as It Is
Confessed in the Nicene-Constantinopolitan Creed (381)* (Faith and Order Paper 153) (Geneva:
World Council of Churches, 1991) 2–3.

is seen as a privileged expression of the essential nucleus of the apostolic faith. Before examining the individual articles of the Creed, the Faith and Order study defines the concept of apostolic faith to which is due a key function.

> The term *apostolic faith* used in this study does not refer to a single fixed formula, nor to a specific moment in Christian history. Rather, it points to the dynamic reality of the Christian faith. The faith is grounded in the prophetic witness of the people of the Old Testament, and in the normative testimony, reflected in the New Testament, of the apostles and those who proclaimed together with them the gospel in the early days (apostolic age) and in the testimony of their community. The apostolic faith is expressed in confession, in preaching, in worship and in the sacraments of the Church as well as in the creedal statements, decisions of councils and confessional texts and in the life of the Church.[19]

The concept of apostolic faith lends to freeing dialogue from the conditioning of a reductive biblicism. It surely does not intend to question the value of Scripture as the fundamental norm of the faith of the church and, therefore, of the dialogue among the churches. Instead, the history of the ecumenical movement documents that the common hearing of the biblical witness and the force to interpret it together in many cases are revealed decisive factors in the search of consensus. Nevertheless, Scripture cannot be isolated from the ecclesial community that interprets it and from within the historical process—the tradition—in which the biblical message has been transmitted. The formulas "apostolic faith" and the "faith of the Church through the ages" intends, however, to underline the normativity of the beginning—the apostolic element—and together the continuity and the coherence of the transmission—the faith of the church through the ages—implicated in the promise made to the church that it will not fail until the fulfillment of the kingdom. On the other hand, the importance of the process of tradition, considered as a whole, does not only not exclude, but demands the exact verification of the continuity and coherence with the beginning of tradition on the basis of precise criteria. These criteria allow for discernment of what is permanently normative and what is instead only the fruit of historical contingencies.

The Creed also offers a paradigm of the internal articulation of the content of apostolic faith. If this scheme is maintained in the background,

---

[19] Ibid., n. 7, pp. 2–3.

it can be affirmed that ecumenical dialogue directed to reconstruct consensus in the confession of faith has not considered faith in the Father, in the Son, and in the Holy Spirit in a direct way. Concerning trinitarian faith, the churches committed to the ecumenical movement today share the inheritance of the early church. Also, dissent over christology with the ancient Oriental Orthodox churches that had not accepted the christological formulas of the Councils of Ephesus and Chalcedon is to be upheld since it was possible that a different theological terminology intended to express the same faith.

A simple statistical survey shows that contemporary ecumenical dialogue primarily deals with the understanding of the church and the sacraments. To this focus, doubtless the most commonplace one, is added that of theological anthropology that saw the comparison on matters related to the doctrine of justification and on the way in which divine grace acts in the believer. The principal ground on which ecumenical dialogue is involved in the reconstruction of consensus is, therefore, represented by the third article of the Creed and concerns in particular the work of the Spirit, which actualizes in time the salvation given once and for all by Christ, and the instruments—the church and the sacraments—to the service of such actualization and communication of salvation. Significant results are registered on both themes.

At the center of polemics between Lutherans and Catholics since the sixteenth century, the doctrine of justification refers to an essential aspect of the conception of Christian salvation but has also assumed the symbolic value of synthetic expression of confessional identity and has therefore been considered the root from which is born all the divergences between Catholics and Protestants. Despite the weight of this historical heredity, the results achieved on this point are very meaningful, thanks also to the development taken place in Catholic and Evangelical theology. Launched in the 1960s, bilateral dialogue has in fact been able to ascertain that many motives for dissent were already surpassed, and dealt with gathering and deepening the results of biblical exegesis and of studies of the history of dogma. In the survey of recent ecumenical dialogue, the doctrine of justification does not only represent one theme upon which it is possible to reach ample theological consensus, but it also constitutes the most advanced point of official reception of dialogue in which the Roman Catholic Church has participated. After work that lasted more than thirty years, and after intense discussion, not without internal tensions within the churches, on October 31, 1999, the *Joint Declaration on the Doctrine of Justification* was signed,[20] in which it is affirmed that the Roman Catholic Church and the Lutheran churches are "now able to articulate a common understanding of our justification by God's grace through faith in Christ" and that, thanks to this consensus, "the remaining differences in its explication are no longer the occasion for doctrinal condemnations."[21]

Regarding the understanding of the church, dialogue has also made possible the achievement of meaningful results. Particularly within Faith and Order, dialogue has gone on giving precisely the ecclesiological picture that has inspired the activity of the WCC and is proposed in the whole ecumenical movement. Currently, the concept of *communion (koinonia)* represents the synthetic figure of the vision of the church that is taking shape and that finds consensus in bilateral dialogues and in vast sectors of theological reflection, which at times makes a use of it that is rather flexible and open to interpretations that are not always compatible. An illustration of the contents of the notion of communion is found in the document *The Nature and Purpose of the Church*, published by Faith and Order in November 1998, in which is offered a provisional report of the study project in progress on ecclesiology. The fundamental dimensions of ecclesial communion are indicated in the document.

> It is only by virtue of God's gift of grace through Jesus Christ that deep, lasting communion is made possible; by faith and baptism, persons participate in the mystery of Christ's death, burial and resurrection. United to Christ, though the Holy Spirit, they are thus joined to all who are "in Christ": they belong to the new communion—the new community—of the risen Lord [. . .]. Visible and tangible signs of the new life of communion are expressed in receiving and sharing the faith of the apostles; breaking and sharing the eucharistic bread; praying with, and for one another and for the needs of the world; serving one another in love."[22]

In bilateral dialogues, reflection on the church and on the sacraments concentrates on the issues that are specifically controversial

---

[20] Lutheran-Roman Catholic Joint Commission, *Joint Declaration on the Doctrine of Justification*, Document 44 in "XXI. Lutheran-Roman Catholic Dialogue," in Gros, Meyer and Rusch, *Growth in Agreement II*, 566–82. For a comprehensive presentation of the ecumenical dialogue on justification, cf. A. Maffeis, *Giustificazione. Percorsi teologici nel dialogo tra le chiese* (Cinisello Balsamo [MI]: Edizioni Paoline, 1998).

[21] *Joint Declaration*, n. 5.

[22] *The Nature and Purpose of the Church: A Stage on the Way to a Common Statement* (Faith and Order Paper 181) (Geneva: World Council of Churches, 1998) nn. 55–56.

among the confessions. It is not possible here to examine in a detailed way the results reached on the various themes. Altogether, it can be affirmed that there are advances delineating a substantial consensus on the understanding of the local church and of its constitutive elements: proclamation, sacraments, and ministries. Significant results have also been reached on the thorny issue of ordained ministry. This has been possible because the rigid opposition has been overcome between a priesthood fixed in the celebration of the sacraments and a ministry of the Word; that is, a function of proclamation, and a presidency of the celebration of the sacraments and guide of the community so organically integrated in the pastoral office. Just the same, dialogue is not left held captive by the alternative between the use or still less by the concept of sacrament to define ordination. It has been able to ascertain that there is a substantial convergence in the understanding of the act by which ministry is conferred: with the imposition of hands and the prayer is communicated a gift of the Spirit that qualifies in a permanent way the exercise of ecclesial ministry.[23] Some unresolved matters related to the structure of universal communion still remain, however, such as the significance of the episcopate and the historic continuity in the transmission of ministry (apostolic succession), of the authority of the magisterium due the church, and the primacy of the Bishop of Rome. Also on these themes there are, nevertheless, elements of convergence that allow the churches born from the Reformation to affirm that the recovery of the sign of the historical continuity in the transmission of the office is desirable and to recognize the principle according to which the universal unity of the church requires appropriate structures in the service of communion.

The proposal formulated by John Paul II in the encyclical *Ut Unum Sint* (1995) takes up an issue given attention by the dialogues. In the document he speaks about the question put to him "to find a way of exercising the primacy which, while in no way renouncing what is essential to its mission, is nonetheless open to a new situation" (n. 95). He invited church leaders and theologians to a dialogue on this topic to explore the possibilities of a revision that dares to make effective for all Christians the service of unity the Bishop of Rome intends to fulfill. The invitation of John Paul II has received responses from theologians

---

[23] On these themes, cf. A. Maffeis, *Il ministero nella chiesa: uno studio del dialogo cattolico-luterano (1967–1984)* (Pontificia Università Gregoriana: Dissertatio Series Romana 2), Gorgonzola (Milano: Glossa, 1991).

and representatives of different Christian churches and has revived the debate that in preceding decades had been launched in ecumenical dialogues and within the churches.

The resumption of the discussion of various views has resulted in ascertaining a growing consensus around the value of a ministry of unity in service to the universal church analogous to what is found on other levels of the church. Many also recognize how such an office cannot be created anew but can only be an institution as that of the primacy of the Bishop of Rome that in history has in fact exercised a role of this kind. Such recognition is encouraged, then, by the availability expressed by *Ut Unum Sint* to distinguish in the ministry of the Bishop of Rome what is essential from the dogmatic point of view and what is simply derived from historical contingency. For the Catholic tradition, the meaning to be attributed to the dogmatic and juridical form in which primacy has been defined by Vatican I remains an open issue. Such precision, in fact, took place without the participation of other churches and within an ecclesiology of the perfect society that impoverishes the inheritance of the first millennium. The Catholic Church asks other Christian traditions at what point are they disposed to join in the recognition of the Bishop of Rome, not only as the symbolic function of the personification of ecclesial unity and the spokesperson of the church, but also as an authority that allows for effectively serving the unity of the universal church.[24]

One Faith and Different Theologies

In the history of the ecumenical movement, the admonition not to confuse ecclesial unity with an absolute uniformity of doctrines and structures returns with insistence. Such a way to understand the goal of ecumenical effort would not only be unrealistic, but it is also in contradiction with the model of the primitive church. The New Testament, in fact, gives witness to the one Lord in plural form, using different expressions and theological languages. Equally, the writings of the New Testament reveal the presence of notable differences in the ministries and the organization of community life, and they do not permit reverting back to the structural uniformity that is only subsequently affirmed. On the other hand, the same primitive communities witness

[24] On the state of dialogue regarding the ministry of the Bishop of Rome, cf. A. Maffeis, "Il ministero di unità per la Chiesa universale nei colloqui ecumenici," in A. Acerbi, ed., *Il ministero del Papa in prospettiva ecumenica* (Milano: Vita e Pensiero, 1999) 233–75.

to the profound conscience to form the one church of Christ. They had such instruments that allowed for mutual recognition and exchange of members and ministries. Only in this way can the process of formation in the New Testament canon through which the traditions proper to the individual churches have been shared and gathered together in one body be explained. Such a process is highly significant from the ecclesiological point of view because it reflects an ecclesial environment in which unity in faith is affirmed through the exchange of respective traditions and the delimitation of a corpus of normative writings, without however carrying out any fusion but respecting its originality.

As in all ages of church history, in the contemporary ecumenical movement the concrete application of the principle of unity in plurality is not at all peaceful. The paths of those who agree on recognizing the validity of the principle divide when it comes to specifying what conditions are absolutely necessary for the unity of the church and what differences can be maintained without compromising unity. In fact, the line of demarcation between the two spheres is traced in ways rather diverse according to the ecclesial vision from which one departs. It must not be forgotten, then, that historical divisions among the churches have been determined specifically to manifest an unsurpassable dissent regarding what must be held essential for the faith of the church and for its structures.

In order to reach a "consensual" application of the principle of unity in diversity, ecumenical dialogue has put into effect a process of deepened discernment of tradition. Not all that has been inherited from the past (doctrine, institutions, practices) belongs to the tradition in the strict sense; that is, that it embodies essential elements of the Gospel transmitted in history that in no way can get lost.[25] The search for consensus in the expression of the apostolic faith necessarily, therefore, passes through the critical sieve of the forms in which the faith has been witnessed to and lived in history. It does this to distinguish the

---

[25] The Fourth World Conference on Faith and Order (Montreal, 1963) deepened the theme and it proposed the distinction between the Tradition (upper case "T") and the traditions (lower case "t"): "By the *Tradition* is meant the Gospel itself, transmitted from generation to generation in and by the Church, Christ himself present in the life of the Church. By *tradition* is meant the traditionary process. The term *traditions* is used in two senses, to indicate both the diversity of forms of expression and also what we call confessional traditions, for instance, the Lutheran tradition or the Reformed tradition." Rodger, P. C. and Vischer, Lukas. *The Fourth World Conference on Faith and Order, Montreal 1963* (Faith and Order Paper 42) (Geneva/London: World Council of Churches/SCM Press, 1964) Section II, "Scripture, Tradition and Traditions," n. 39, p. 50.

essential from the contingent, that is, what is normative for the church of all times and what are possible different options.

In the realization of this discernment, the rediscovery of Scripture as a fundamental norm of the faith represented a decisive factor. In fact, it is a witness of the constitutive moment of the tradition and, therefore, offers the basic criteria of discernment. Although every tradition continues to read the Scripture departing from its own propositions, it can be said that the effort of the common reading of the sacred text made by Christians of diverse confessions constituted a deciding factor in the development of the ecumenical movement. Owing to this, it is possible to overcome the apologetic attitude, which in the defense of one's own confessional position was a hindrance, and to find a common point of reference. Still, prior to ecumenical dialogue, this common reading developed on the exegetical level. Before anywhere else, confessional barriers collapsed in this area, and scholars of the different churches were found side by side, engaged in a common enterprise. More than an explicitly ecumenical intent, to unite the efforts of exe-getes was the convergence in the method followed and, in particular, the fact of finding oneself at work on common ground delimited by the application of the historical-critical method. Served by a method that puts the dogmatic-confessional "prejudice" in parentheses, exegesis has made available to theology an interpretation of Scripture that can garner a consensus most extensive in comparison to that limited by the individual confessions.

Assuming the results of the exegetical work, the theological reflection has also been able to make worthwhile in a way more effective and coherent the principle according to which "the study of the 'sacred page' ought to be the very soul of theology" (*DV* 24), and the Scripture constitutes the fundamental norm of theological discourse. Without reducing itself to pure repetition of the biblical formulas, ecumenical consensus has in many cases been formulated by closely tracing the language of Scripture. It, in fact, contains resources able to overcome incurable opposition among the terminologies developed within particular confessions and that often are irremediably conditioned by the polemic of finality that inspired it. An example of this way of proceeding is found in the Lutheran-Roman Catholic dialogue in the USA. It formulates a basic consensus concerning the doctrine of justification in a language inspired by the apostle Paul and in a style close to that of the confession of faith: "our entire hope of justification and salvation rests on Christ Jesus and on the gospel whereby the good news of God's merciful action in Christ is made known; we do not place our ultimate trust in anything other than God's promise and saving work in Christ."[26]

Also in the search for consensus in eucharistic faith, biblical language in some cases is revealed decisive with the purpose to overcome the oppositions inherited from the past. Regarding the Eucharist, the document of Lima, published in 1982 by Faith and Order, affirms: "Christ himself with all that he has accomplished for us and for all creation (in his incarnation, servanthood, ministry, teaching, suffering, sacrifice, resurrection, ascension and sending of the Spirit) is present in this anamnesis, granting us communion with himself."[27] The concept of memorial thereby becomes the point of encounter that makes sense of the opposing demands that, in the course of history, are manifested in the elaboration of Eucharist doctrine: it allows for reconciling the uniqueness of the sacrifice of Christ with the real and effective character of his presence and the gift of salvation received in the sacrament.

The reference to Scripture, in particular to the manifold forms in which the Christian message is set forth in the New Testament, has been important for dialogue also from another point of view. We have already noted that in these writings the Gospel message is formulated with different categories, and that the one faith finds expression in a multiplicity of theological languages. If this is valid for the church of its origins, it can be presumed that the faith can legitimately have different expressions in following ages. Reasons for the plurality of theological languages are varied, but they all are somehow tied up to the *historicity* of the confession of faith and the historically conditioned character of language in which they find expression. To realize its own mission to proclaim the Gospel in the time when it finds itself alive, the church must assume the language of the contemporary culture. The choice of an expressive means effective in communicating the faith in a given historical moment, however, also involves acceptance of the perspective that it implies and, therefore, of the limit such a perspective inevitably carries. Acceptance of the ontological Greek language has allowed the early church to formulate its faith in a comprehensible way within

---

[26] *Justification by Faith*, in "Lutheran-Roman Catholic Dialogues," in Joseph A. Burgess and Jeffrey Gros, F.S.C, eds. *Building Unity: Ecumenical Dialogues with Roman Catholic Participation in the United States* [1965–1986]. (Ecumenical Documents IV) (New York/Mahwah, N.J.: Paulist Press, 1989) Introduction §4, p. 218.

[27] *BEM* II, n. 6. Cf. also *Eucharistic Doctrine (Windsor Statement) 1971*, ¶5 in "Anglican-Roman Catholic Conversations," in Meyer and Vischer, *Growth in Agreement*, 70; *The Eucharist: Final Report of the Joint Roman Catholic-Lutheran Commission, 1978*, ¶17 in "Lutheran-Roman Catholic Conversations," in Meyer and Vischer, *Growth in Agreement*, 196.

that cultural horizon and to defend it from deformation. It has also brought with it the loss of some characteristic accentuations of biblical language.

The ecclesial separations occurred when some divergences had been judged incompatible with ecclesial communion. They are coupled to the rupture because the attempt to come to a common discernment failed (in the colloquies of religion of the sixteenth century), or were not even undertaken (in the case of the relationships between the Latin church and the Byzantine church). The break once consumed, each ecclesial community made its own discernment of the tradition, with the consequence that to the inevitable historical and prospective character of the confession of faith is also added the taking of polemical distance from other expressions of the faith and other communities in which they had risen. From this state of things is derived an impoverishment because theology, enlisted for fighting heresies, has offered a reductive and partial reading of the tradition that accented the elements of distinction and forgot common patrimony. In this regard, the description given in 1937 by Y. Congar of the processes that are determined in the Catholic Church following the condemnation of doctrinal errors remains relevant today.

> Whenever error is expressed on a given point, the body of the church stiffens itself, its strength polarizes in order to resist evil; before false affirmation that is . . . the provocation of the truth, true affirmation is affirmed and specified; in most cases dogma on the whole is satisfied to give greater relief and greater precision to truth that is underestimated or denied by error; so if error is always partial, the contrary dogmatic truth risks also being partial (in the measure in which it is limited at being contrary truth; the Scholastics say the contrary ones are of the same kind). Those who for temperament or system or convenience question official texts more than life; the theologians who are lazy and at times opportunist who prefer to do no more than open their Denzinger rather than study the scriptures, the fathers, the liturgy and the lived faith of the church and the positive witness of Christian sense; the apologists, finally, who by profession are approved to fight the errors of the day and draw the church to extremes; in short, the majority, at least the majority of those who speak, write and make themselves heard, set against error a hardened truth, which is incomplete if it stops at a formulation that is unilateral and partial.[28]

---

[28] Y Congar, *Chrétiens désunis: principes d'un "œcuménisme" catholique* (Unam Sanctam 1) (Paris: Éditions du Cerf, 1937) 34–35. [Transator's note: The English translation uses the

The effort undertaken by ecumenical dialogue to discern the tradition is not exhausted in the search of formulations capable of expressing common faith in an adequate way. Also posed is the question of meaning that, in light of the rediscovery of the common faith, is assumed by the doctrines and forms of Christian life that developed over the centuries in mutual opposition within the separate communities. In fact, it is not a matter of simple school opinions, but of considerable parts of the normative teaching of the church and of elements that contribute in a decisive way to define the confessional identity of these communities. The developing debate in bilateral dialogues has placed in question a presupposition tacitly received at the beginning of the ecumenical movement, that the churches must abandon their own "confessional" identity in order to find a new "ecumenical" identity. In the bilateral dialogues, it has been above all the Lutheran churches that vindicate the permanent value of confessional identity: since this is based on the affirmation of an authentic aspect of the Gospel, it must be able to be maintained. At the same time, the necessity is recognized to liberate confessional patrimony from its unilateral character. This allows it to rediscover its "ecumenical communion." To this end, what must be realized is what Harding Meyer called a "redefinition of the confessions in dialogue"; that is, a process that allows for overcoming the unilateralities, the reductions, and the polemical accentuations that make the different confessions unacceptable in the form in which they exist today. In this way, confessional identity rediscovers its proper and authentic form and becomes acceptable as a legitimate expression of the one Christian faith.[29]

Therefore, if dialogue pursues the objective to reach a common formulation of faith, it subsequently makes us ask if the consensus reached on the fundamental aspects are capable of sustaining the different historical forms in which Christian faith has been understood and lived in the particular ecclesial traditions. In this way, positions that in the past seemed irreconcilable today could be held as legitimately different theological explanations of the same apostolic faith.

---

original French and the Italian of Maffeis. Y. Congar, *Divided Christendom: A Catholic Study of the Problem of Reunion* (London: Geoffrey Bles, 1939); the English translation of *Chrétiens désunis*, does not have the full text as it appears in the French original or in the Italian of Maffeis; see 29–30 of the English translation.]

[29] Cf. H. Meyer, "«Einheit in versöhnter verschiedenheit»–«konziliare Gemeinschaft»–«organische Union», Gemeinsamkeit und Differenz gegenwärtig diskutierter Einheitkonzeptionen," in *Ökumenische Rundschau* 27 (1978) 387–89.

In speaking of particular issues, bilateral dialogues have verified the practicability of this model that establishes the goal of a *differentiated consensus*. Signed by Catholics and Lutherans, the *Joint Declaration on the Doctrine of Justification* presents this structure of consensus in a particularly clear form. In the central part of the document a common affirmation of faith is followed by the explanation of the forms in which the Catholic and Lutheran traditions have expressed their understanding of Christian salvation. Concerning the known problem of the forensic or effective character of justification, the declaration expresses itself in these terms.

> We confess together that God forgives sin by grace and at the same time frees human beings from sin's enslaving power and imparts the gift of new life in Christ. When persons come by faith to share in Christ, God no longer imputes to them their sin and through the Holy Spirit effects in them an active love. These two aspects of God's gracious action are not to be separated, for persons are by faith united with Christ, who in his person is our righteousness (1 Cor 1:30): both are forgiven of sin and the saving presence of God himself. Because Catholics and Lutherans confess this together, it is true to say that: When Lutherans emphasize that the righteousness of Christ is our righteousness before God in Christ through the declaration of forgiveness and that only in union with Christ is one's life renewed. . . . When Catholics emphasize the renewal of the interior person through the reception of grace imparted as a gift to the believer . . . they wish to insist that God's forgiving grace always brings with a gift of new life, which in the Holy Spirit becomes effective in active love.[30]

So as to not misunderstand the sense of these and other affirmations of the declaration, it must be remembered that the compatibility among positions held irreconcilable in the past is not simply postulated without proof. The text defers to exegetical and historical studies that can ascertain in an analytical way what is affirmed synthetically. Similarly, it is suggested that the compatibility of confessional positions calls for a hermeneutic that intentionally explains them in the sense of common affirmation and takes account of the appeal the contrasted doctrine bears. In other words, it remains possible to continue to read Lutheran or Catholic confessional affirmation in such ways to make them be held irreconcilable. What the declaration intends to say is that it is also possible to read confessional affirmations in the sense of common affirmation, and this the signatory churches are committed to do.

[30] *Joint Declaration*, nn. 22–24.

Chapter 4

A Dialogue among the Churches

In the preceding chapter, the illustration of the constitutive elements of dialogue allowed for recognizing the connection of this method to the communicative structure of the church. This datum has then become more profound, paying attention in a particular way to the essential content of the communication that takes place in the church and among the churches. Such content is constituted by the apostolic faith, professed, celebrated, and lived together, and represents the base of ecclesial communion. In this last chapter, our reflection continues with the intention to complete the delineated picture, especially by highlighting the implications of the choice of the dialogical method made by the individuals involved. We will try to indicate on what conditions real dialogue can be realized; what attitudes the interlocutors must assume; in what relationship are those who are directly involved in the search for the formulation of the consensus with the churches represented by them; what mutual recognition allows the churches to undertake dialogue; and what destination they intend to reach by taking this path.

Conditions for an Authentic Dialogue

Both daily experience and the history of the ecumenical movement show that dialogue is hardly a fruit that spontaneously grows on the tree of manifold interpersonal relationships. It constitutes the point of arrival of an often fatiguing journey realized only if precise conditions are given to which people and churches can indeed encounter one another. The possibility by which a genuine dialogue is realized depends, therefore, on a delicate equilibrium of relationships and factors and can be compromised when a condition is lacking or one of the elements does not work in the way it should. Reflecting on the principal obstacles that impede encounter and mutual understanding, Y. Congar affirms that "dialogue has two major enemies, monologue and confusion."[1] Clearly, monologue is situated at the extreme opposite of dialogue and denotes the incapacity of relationship, but also the simple speaking in the presence of others not necessarily equivalent to dialogue. Because this is realized, it is necessary that the interlocutors are able to synchronize speaking and listening. Otherwise "confusion" is the inevitable consequence of the overlapping of discourse that does not find a hearing in the audience to which the word is addressed.

In the literature that draws on the history and method of ecumenical research, innumerable indications, more or less concrete and detailed, are found on the attitudes and conditions that make dialogue possible. Such indications habitually apply valid principles for human communication in general to the relationships among the churches. Beyond the multiplicity of detailed indications, one can nevertheless individualize a fundamental presupposition on which the possibility of dialogue radically depends: the interlocutors must recognize each other in their *alterity* and together be disposed to go outside of themselves in order to encounter each other on a common ground. When recognition of the alterity of the interlocutor is missing, or because one is closed in on oneself and refuses relationships, or because one establishes a "fusional" type of relation that effaces the distinction of individuals, at best an appearance of dialogue can be had. Dialogue demands, therefore, as the necessary condition for its execution, the opening to the other in his or her being and the availability of listening to the word with which one reveals oneself and seeks recognition. When this condition is lacking, what is had is appearance, and what is being called dialogue is in reality monologue. Equally, dialogue also degenerates when the one speaking lacks fidelity to self, to one's own identity that constitutes one as "other" for interlocutors.

Illustrating the structure of dialogue, in the preceding chapter we underlined that the objective of dialogue is to reach a consensus. However, this purpose cannot be pursued with any means. At the base of dialogue is found a precise option about the way the desired consen-

---

[1] Y. Congar, *Ecumenism and the Future of the Church* (Chicago: Priory Press, 1967) 50.

sus is reached: accord cannot be sought after by means that deny the freedom and the dignity of the interlocutors. In fact, where relationships are conditioned by violence, or an asymmetry is determined that puts people or groups in a condition of subjection regarding others, the possibility of dialogue is compromised to the root. Because there is dialogue, all the individual participants must recognize themselves reciprocally as interlocutors with equal rights and must accept that each one can freely make one's own conviction be heard and defend one's own interests.[2]

Linked to this fundamental option are some *expectations* that, always implicitly and sometimes explicitly, are presupposed by those who undertake dialogue. The interlocutors hope that all express what they indeed think, that they do not want to be reciprocally tricked, but that they be *truthful*, that is, that they express themselves in a way coherent with their very selves. Furthermore, they hope that all can speak the *truth*, that is, express themselves in a way corresponding to the matter being dealt with so that it would be possible to verify the correspondence of affirmations to reality. Equally essential are the expectations that all the interlocutors express themselves *comprehensibly* to one another so that an effective relationship among them can be established that all conduct themselves *justly*, that is, that they observe the rules of the language, norms, customs, and expressions of acceptable common behavior, so as to act in a way suitable to the situation.[3]

Dialogue, therefore, in the first place demands that in personal relationships a fundamental attitude oriented to recognition and respect of the freedom of the interlocutor is assumed. Still, at the same time, dialogue has a fundamental reference to truth that constitutes the norm for verifying the quality of communication. The two aspects must be maintained in strict correlation. As the background disposition in relationships with interlocutors, the dialogical attitude prevents a misuse of the method as a means to deceitfully pursue the affirmation of self. On the other hand, the orientation of dialogue to the search of truth preserves it from dissipating itself in a state together full of good intentions

---

[2] Cf. K. O. Apel, *Etica della comunicazione* (Milano: Jaca Book, 1992) 29–31.

[3] Cf. M. Kehl, *La Chiesa*, 132–34; the author takes his inspiration from the thesis of K. O. Apel. He also re-proposes the conviction of the German philosopher according to which the presence of these expectations, which never adequately corresponds to reality, confers a "utopian" structure upon human communication and a necessary orientation toward an "ideal community of communication" that is a condition for historical attempts to communicate; cf. ibid., 134–35.

but empty or in care of the quality of personal relationships that become ends in themselves.

The effort to create and maintain the conditions mentioned is evident in the different initiatives of ecumenical dialogue described in the previous chapters. The first step the churches must take in beginning the path of reconciliation was the renouncement of the polemical attitude to establish a relationship of trust. Mutual listening has so permitted to discover that the other "real" was different from the other "imagined." The study of the official documents and of theology, however accurate and honest, is not in a position to open the access to the totality of the faith and ecclesial experience of the other communities. Only mutual listening and the effort to understand, based on the trust granted the witness that each one gives regarding the reasons of one's faith, allows the discovery of the vital world of the interlocutor.

This process is not exhausted in the mutual knowledge obtained through the comparison of convictions and practices, a comparison based on the trust granted the explanations each is able to give of the positions of one's own tradition. According to J. Famerée, ecumenical dialogue is an itinerary of mutual progressive discovery that must not stop at the surface but must explore the depths.

> Until now it is limited to conscious theological positions. But even at this level of church leaders and experts consideration must also be given to the unspoken and to the confessional unconscious (doctrinal, cultural, historical . . .) which impinges upon dialogue. We are not referring here to individual psychological blocks but to a collective psychology, partially unaware, to that which we have called the mental morphology or cultural typology which belongs to each Christian confession: each is bearer of a confessionally oriented Christian anthropology.[4]

Solution of conflict is not possible if the unspoken does not emerge and if it is not brought to a level of rational, verbal dialogue. What is not brought to a level of consciousness and is not dealt with openly but has been repressed re-presents itself at the earliest opportunity to pollute relationships without it being possible to clearly determine the cause of the felt uneasiness. The recourse to psychoanalytical categories (the unconscious, repression) to describe the processes ecumenical dialogue

---

[4] J. Famerée, "De l'affrontement à la reconaissance. Petite «phénoménologie» du dialogue oecuménique," in *Ephemerides Theologicae Lovanienses* 74 (1998) 356. Cf. also G. R. Evans, *Method in Ecumenical Theology: The Lessons So Far* (Cambridge: Cambridge University Press, 1996) 23–30.

sets up and the risks to avoid is not casual. This language alludes to a kind of collective psychology belonging to each Christian tradition, whose complexity and historical roots must be adequately known. The sedimentations in the ecclesial conscience and in the praxis of a history marked by conflict must indeed be recognized as such and can be exceeded only with a demeanor that coherently pursues the purpose of reestablishing conditions of mutual trust.

An Ecumenical Theology

Language represents the fundamental means thanks to which interpersonal communication and encounter is possible. Nevertheless, at the disposal of the interlocutors the linguistic means does not perfectly correspond to the intention of the communicator. Without a doubt, it presents a certain pliancy that allows the user to modify it to better serve the way one expresses oneself. From this point of view, "style" is nothing other than the personal imprint given to the expressed language and form that the individual shares with other members of the community. The transformation of language, however, only happens within certain limits. When these are surpassed, it falls into the equivocal, and communication fails due to the lack of shared codes. The limited suppleness of language indeed depends on the fact that the meaning of the terms and the grammatical rules must have a sufficient stability to allow communication among the members of the community using it. Furthermore, every language carries in itself the traces of the past, of the culture that has produced it and of the use that communities more or less vast have made of it for centuries. Precisely because it is not an original creation of an individual but the common patrimony of a community that extends itself in space and time, language enables communication among different people. For the same reason, however, no one can arrange in an exclusive way or arbitrarily modify its meanings and rules.

Since the beginning, prominent figures of ecumenical dialogue have found themselves in the rather unenviable situation of having received the task to look for agreement on matters subject to controversy among the churches. Yet they must discharge such a task using a language produced, or at least profoundly conditioned, precisely by the controversy they want to overcome. In fact, the language of controversy has not only conditioned the perception of the other churches, but it has also profoundly marked the formulation each church has given to its own faith. In many cases, this faith has found expression with the more or less explicit intent of delimitation in comparison to the position of the adversary. An evident confirmation of this is found in Catholic theology following the Council of Trent that precisely accented aspects the Reformers had contested. The doctrine of grace is so structured around the concept of created grace (against a "forensic" conception of justification understood as imputation of a justice that remains external to the human person). Eucharistic doctrine placed the accent on the sacrificial dimension. The theology of ordination defined ecclesial ministry as a priesthood oriented to the celebration of the eucharistic sacrifice. The presence of speculative positions can be found in Protestant theology that suffer the same limits as those they intended to reject.

Despite intending to travel different paths from those of the past, ecumenical dialogue does not represent a totally new beginning. In fact, it cannot avoid encountering issues that determined ecclesial separation in the past, and, therefore, it is forced to take up the terminology in which the problems had been formulated when dissent was manifested. On the other hand, dialogue has some hope for success only if it shows a sufficient creativity to open paths of understanding and to find new language for faith where in the past positions seemed irreconcilable. To realize this goal, ecumenical dialogue has made the effort to set up communication between the traditional languages of the churches, and it has tried to create the conditions so that they can mutually understand one another. Decisive in this initiative is the application of the principle elaborated by historical science for the interpretation of the documents and the witness of the past. Thanks to the resources of hermeneutics, it is possible to contextualize doctrine and practice and gather the intention underlying formulations that in their immediacy seem irreconcilable.

In this work of common discernment of the tradition and of the language of controversy, ecumenical dialogue has chosen to apply a "hermeneutics of confidence" translated in the disposability to give credit to the positive intention declared by the interlocutor in the explanation of what belongs to his or her ecclesial tradition.[5] Such hermeneu-

---

[5] "As the churches engage in dialogue in the growing communion of churches in the ecumenical movement, a further and wider hermeneutical community is created. As it engages in ecumenical dialogue each church and tradition opens itself to being interpreted by other churches and traditions. To listen to the other does not necessarily mean to accept what other churches say, but to reckon with the possibility that the Spirit speaks within and through the others. This might be called 'hermeneutics of confidence,'" *A Treasure in Earthen Vessels: An Instrument for an Ecumenical Reflection on Hermeneutics* (Faith and Order Paper 182) (Geneva: World Council of Churches, 1998) n. 8, p. 10.

tics is not founded upon the arbitrary supposition that all positions have equal value. By this method, affirmation of their compatibility is surely reached, but at the cost of their capacity to speak the truth. This is based instead on what a recent text of Faith and Order devoted to the theme of hermeneutics called the principle of the "right intention of faith."

> Hermeneutics in the service of unity must also proceed on the presumption that those who interpret the Christian tradition differently each have "right intention of faith." It is not only a condition of dialogue, but a fruitful product of dialogue, that the partners come to appreciate and trust one another's sincerity and good intention . . . [6]

Nevertheless, a hermeneutics of confidence must not be confused with a naivety that would end up incapable of garnering the real differences, let alone with an attitude that considers irrelevant the moves for dissent. The same Faith and Order document underlines the necessity that a hermeneutics of confidence be accompanied by a "hermeneutics of coherence" capable of demonstrating the real compatibility and complementarity that affirm the different traditions, and by the "hermeneutics of suspicion" capable of unmasking the ideological use of arguments for justifying unsustainable positions.

The first phase of the encounter, therefore, has as its goal to arrive at an understanding of the language of the interlocutor and to recognize it as a viable way to express Christian faith. The will to realize this effort is not quite discounted because theologians and believers often feel truly at ease with the confessional horizon in which they find themselves and in which they have learned the language of faith. In fact, such a horizon offers precise points of reference and delimits a world family one does not feel the need to abandon, especially if the experience of the encounter with Christians who belong to other confessions is rare or entirely absent. The effort achieved by ecumenical dialogue, especially the bilaterals, is directed to make it understood that the access to the most vast ecumenical horizon does not involve the loss, let alone the betrayal, of one's own confessional horizon. A confessional horizon is, rather, recognized in its legitimacy, while at the same time

---

[6] *A Treasure in Earthen Vessels*, n. 30, p. 22. The formula "right intention of faith" takes its inspiration from the Document of Lima (1982) in the section on ministry regarding the differences existing among the churches on the significance of apostolic succession: "Churches in ecumenical conversations can recognize their respective ordained ministries if they are mutually assured of their intention to transmit the ministry of the Word and sacrament in continuity with apostolic times"; *BEM*, Ministry 5.

it discovers its particular partiality and the necessity to be broadened and enriched.[7]

Theological work that ends in the context of ecumenical dialogue also pursues a second objective, that is, the elaboration of a common language that allows for confessing the faith together. In this way, the foundation upon which is based the recognition of the legitimacy of different ways of expressing the one faith is ensured and the foundation for the development of a common tradition is set. This effort is as necessary as that of having the different confessional perspectives communicate with each other. Reasoning founded upon the legitimacy and the compatibility of what they affirm, in fact, demands "to find a way for everyone to be sure that it is the same truth which is being referred to."[8] This equivalence, however, cannot be established unless it passes through a common language and an expression of faith upon which there can be agreement. Despite being entirely legitimate, insistence on the plurality of expressions of faith cannot be, therefore, the only and ultimate criterion of ecumenical dialogue. With equal force it is necessary to underline the demand of implicit unity in the confession of faith. Precisely for its capacity to speak the believed truth with the same words, it represents the visible sign of the bond that unites believers and churches.

Ecumenical theology intends to pursue these objectives. The allusion to two moments does not have to be understood in a quasi-chronological sense that, once having completed the task of putting the confessional languages in communication, dialogue moves on to the elaboration of a common language. In reality, it deals with the two dimensions that, even with different weight, are always present in every dialogue. On one hand, the reflection developed in dialogue among persons belonging to different churches calls for departing from the narrow space of one's own confessional theology in order to recover an ecumenical horizon. On the other hand, it cannot give up making comprehensible the common language to which the dialogue tries to give form and to show how it does not contradict the conscience of faith of the respective ecclesial communities.

---

[7] Cf. J. T. Ford, "Bilateral Conversations and Denominational Horizons," in *Journal of Ecumenical Studies* 23 (1986) 518–28; G. Pattaro, *Corso di teologia dell'ecumenismo* (Brescia: Queriniana, 1985) 349–57.

[8] G. R. Evans, *Method in Ecumenical Theology*, 89.

Not Doctrine Alone

The privileged attention that we have reserved for the search of unity in the confession of faith ought not effect thinking that the ecumenical movement exhausts itself in theological dialogue and in the search of doctrinal agreement. The places where Christians encounter one another and can seek unity are manifold, and the same confession of faith does not exhaust itself in the most possible exact formulation of revealed truth. Christian faith finds expression in worship. It takes shape in ethics and a spirituality. It lives in a world in which it is called to compare itself with other religions and with all those who intend to promote a more just and peaceful human coexistence. On all these grounds, the Christian confessions face one another and other interlocutors with whom from time to time they have shared goals and projects.

Attention to the practical repercussions of ecclesial life and to social commitment has represented a characteristic of the ecumenical movement since its beginnings. This continuous sensitivity remains alive today and constitutes the reason that greatly prompts initiatives of the World Council of Churches. Defining the area in which ecumenical collaboration is fleshed out on the practical level, the formulation that embraces *peace, justice, and the integrity of creation* has been affirmed in recent years.

In these settings the ecumenical movement has tried first of all to create the conditions for witness and common action on the part of the churches. More recent developments show how Christian commitment in the world is considered by many not merely a part of their ethical responsibility but as an action that assumes a certain ecclesiological value. The realization of concrete projects for the promotion of justice and peace and for the safeguarding of creation has, therefore, been accompanied by a theoretical elaboration directed to the purpose of showing in what way the cause of unity is served by traversing these paths and how the commitment in these fields contributes to defining in a more suitable way the same ecclesial unity the ecumenical movement seeks. The basic conviction is that, together committing themselves in the struggle for justice, in establishing peace, and in the safeguarding of creation, the churches may witness and make historically perceivable the unity and reconciliation offered by God to all humanity.

The theoretical elaboration of the meaning of the "practical" line has sometimes assumed a critical connotation toward the "doctrinal" line traditionally pursued by Faith and Order and shared by the bilateral dialogues. In fact, some hold that concentration on doctrinal matters and on the conditions that allow for reestablishing communion in the celebration of the sacraments unduly narrows the horizon of ecumenical action that must not limit itself to the church but must embrace the world. Illuminating this thought is what Christian Link says when he compares the process of ecclesial unity with a *game* that is played out according to determined rules. Affirmations contained in the confessions of faith develop in the church the same function of the rules that make possible a game, but they are not the same as the game. What is decisive is what is done with the rules, how shape is given to the reality between the picture that defines it, what forms of relationships and what models of behavior they make possible:

> About this it can be asked in critical terms whether in the actual official ecumene if they do not speak primarily of the *rules* instead of the *game*. The game is played on the ground and there happens what is decisive. While some are still concerned about defining the rules, others already *play* the game of the ecumenical church.[9]

Apart from metaphor, the real game of unity is played with the commitment solidly lived by the churches in the world and at the service of the world.

These ideas have been used to interpret the meaning of the so-called "conciliar process," initiated by the Sixth World Assembly of the World Council of Churches (Vancouver, 1983), that intended to involve the churches in reflection and common action on the themes of justice, peace, and the integrity of creation.[10] The document *Costly Unity*,[11] which gathers the results of a consultation organized in 1993 by the World Council of Churches, underlines the necessity to connect

[9] C. Link, *Die Bewegung der Einheit: Gemeinschaft der Kirchen in der Ökumene*, in C. Link, U. Luz, und L. Vischer, *Sie aber hielten fest an der Gemeinschaft . . . Einheit der kirche als Prozeß im Neuen Testament und heute* (Zürich: Benziger–Reinhardt, 1988) 193.

[10] The conciliar process found a synthesis in the world convocation in Seoul (1990); cf. *Now is the Time* (Geneva: World Council of Churches, 1990). We must recall, too, that in Europe the first assembly of the European churches took place in Basel in 1989; cf. A. Filippi, ed., *Basilea: giustizia e pace*, EDB (Bologna, 1989).

[11] Cf. T. Best and W. Granberg-Michaelson, eds., *Costly Unity: Koinonia and Justice, Peace and Creation: A World Council of Churches Consultation on Koinonia and Justice, Peace and Integrity of Creation, Rønde, Denmark, February 24–28, 1993* (Geneva: World Council of Churches Unit III and Unit I, 1993). The discussion continued in two successive consultations (1994 and 1996); the texts of the final reports along with some commentaries may be found in T. Best and M. Robra, eds., *Ecclesiology and Ethics. Ecumenical Ethical Engagement, Moral Formation and the Nature of the Church* (Geneva: World Council of Churches, 1997).

the conciliar process with the dialogue on ecclesial unity conducted by Faith and Order: "The being *(esse)* of the church is at stake in the justice, peace and integrity of creation process. It is not sufficient to affirm that the moral thrust of JPIC [Justice, Peace and the Integrity of Creation] is only *related* to the nature and function of the church."[12] The document states that the concept of *koinonia*, chosen by the WCC as a fundamental ecclesiological category, ultimately must be broadened by the integration of the ethical dimension. In fact, Christian tradition attests the presence of a profound bond between faith and action, between communal life and moral existence. It is certainly not possible to affirm that those who are committed to justice, peace, and the integrity of creation themselves belong to the church. Nevertheless, it can be retained that at work in the common struggle undertaken to promote justice and peace is an *ecclesiogenetic* power able to illuminate the doctrine on the church. Since "the church not only has, but is, a social ethic, a *koinonia* ethic,"[13] the church itself can be defined as a "moral community."

The claim of the importance of an ethical dimension for understanding the church is certainly to be shared. However, it is not always easy to establish how this ecclesial line connects ethical involvement in the world with ecclesial life centered on faith and sacraments. At times one gets the impression that the corrective intention in the comparisons of a conception of the unity of the church forgetful of the Christian responsibility in the world tends insensitively to transform itself into an alternative definition of the same church in which faith and sacraments assume a secondary importance. If, therefore, it is incontestable that the church has received the task of witness and of making historically perceivable the reconciliation offered by God to the world, it must also always pay attention not to reduce ecclesial action to its ethical dimension.

Grassroots Ecumenism

Along with the distinction between "practical" and "doctrinal" ecumenism, there sometimes also appears in the descriptions of the actual ecumenical situation an opposition to ecumenism of the "higher levels" [ai "vertici"] as well as ecumenism on "the ground" [della "base"]. One can perhaps contest a too schematic representation of a more complex reality. But surely the importance of the phenomenon the formula "grassroots ecumenism" alludes to cannot in any way be underestimated. In

---

[12] *Costly Unity*, n. 5.
[13] Ibid., n. 6.

fact, the ecumenical movement has known the development and the diffusion we can observe today only because the ideal of the unity of the church has impassioned more and more groups of faithful who dedicate themselves to sensitizing Christian communities to these themes. In this way, they have prepared favorable ground so that official decisions and results of theological work may be understood and shared.

The development of the ecumenical movement and the fact that it has gained ground in spheres beyond the churches in its turn has determined the increase of the number of individuals who have been made promoters of initiatives in this field at different levels. Although it is easy to realize, it is not, however, guaranteed at the outset that all these individuals agree in pursuing the same objectives. Rather, in recalling themselves to the same ecumenical ideal, in a sensitive way they often establish different priorities of ecumenical action and can follow divergent oaths. The growth of the number of individuals and the richness of their contribution has had, however, as consequence the difficulty in realizing the coordination necessary to assure coherence among the initiatives. More than with an oversimplified opposition of the grass-roots to the higher levels, the ecumenical panorama must, therefore, be represented as a network of individuals who, in a way spontaneous or more institutionalized, with occasional or stable initiatives, commit themselves to promoting dialogue and unity among Christians.

An evident test of the spread and rooting of this ecumenical conscience in more diverse ecclesial setting was had on the occasion of the second European ecumenical meetings, organized at Graz in 1997 by the Conference of European Churches (CEC) and the Council of the European Bishops' Conferences (CCEE).[14] In the narrow sense, the assembly was formed of seven hundred official delegates of the churches who have discussed and approved the documents related to the principal issues the European churches today find themselves facing. The Graz assembly, however, was also an encounter of people. It did not simply deal with a "program for visitors" set at the edges of the working assembly members and proposed to those who did not belong to the official delegations. It consisted of a real and proper assembly that developed parallel to that of the delegates. The number of participants at the open meetings and the outcome of the proposed initiatives had been such that, at least in the perception of the public, they overshad-

---

[14] Cf. *Reconciliation: Gift of God and Source of New Life. Conference of European Churches, 11th Assembly, Graz, Austria, 30 June–4 July 1997* (Geneva: Conference of European Churches, 1998).

owed the role of the official delegations and the editing of the assembly documents.

The Graz meeting thus became a place in which various groups and individuals active in the ecumenical field have begun to speak by presenting their activities and by inviting ecclesial authorities to take up the path of reconciliation with more courage. Particularly in countries where Catholics and Protestants live close to one another, the question of eucharistic hospitality, that is, the possibility, at least in some circumstances, to participate in the Eucharist of another church, is felt in a rather acute way. A remarkable number of the faithful manage to understand with difficulty the obstacles that, according to the judgment of the shepherds of the Catholic Church, prevent participation in another church's Eucharist. Positions on the matter remain remote not primarily on grounds of differences in eucharistic theology, but because on the question of eucharistic hospitality they run into two ways of understanding the relationship between Eucharist and ecclesial unity. On one hand, it appeals back to the tradition of the ancient church to underline that the common participation in the Eucharist presupposes and manifests the existence of full ecclesial communion.[15] Participation in Eucharist in the absence of full ecclesial communion corresponds, therefore, to "simulate" a reality that does not exist, and thereby empties, at least partially, the sign of its meaning. On the other hand, it insists on the fact that the Eucharist is the means that fosters growth in unity and that, at least on some occasions, it must be possible to share the eucharistic meal, since through dialogue the churches have come to discover that they hold in common fundamental elements of Christian faith.[16] On this point dialogue becomes difficult, not only among the

[15] "Yet worship in common is not to be considered as a means to be used indiscriminately for the restoration of Christian unity. There are two main principles governing the practice of such common worship: first, the bearing witness to the unity of the church, and second, the sharing in the meaning of grace. Witness to the unity of the church generally forbids common worship, but the grace to be had from it sometimes commends this practice," *Unitatis Redintegratio*, n. 8. "Its [a sacrament] celebration in a concrete community is the sign of the reality of its unity in faith, worship and community life. As well as being signs, sacraments—most specially the Eucharist—are sources of the unity of the Christian community and of spiritual life, and are means for building them up. Thus Eucharistic communion is inseparably linked to full ecclesial communion and its visible expression," Pontificium Consilium ad Christianorum Unitatem Fovendam, *Directory for the Application of Principles and Norms on Ecumenism* (25 March 1995) (Vatican City: Vatican Press, 1993) n. 129.

[16] "The Reformed churches take the view that, precisely because Christ himself is the host at the table, the church must not impose any obstacles. All those who have received baptism and love the Lord Jesus Christ are invited to the Lord's supper," *Towards*

different traditions, but also within churches, due to the presence of different evaluations of the removal of the obstacles that impede occasional or habitual participation. The problem then is subsequently complicated by the differences remaining in the understanding of the relationship between ordained ministry and the eucharistic celebration, and by the consequences they draw regarding the reciprocity of the admission to Eucharist. The Catholic Church, in fact, on certain conditions, admits the faithful of other churches to the Eucharist (when there is eucharistic faith corresponding to that of the Catholic Church, a spiritual need, and no danger of scandal). But it does not permit its own faithful to participate in the Eucharist of those churches that "have not retained the authentic and full reality of the eucharistic mystery, especially because the sacrament of order is lacking" (*UR* 22).

The families formed by married couples belonging to different confessions are one of the places in which the problem of a common sharing of Eucharist is felt in a most immediate way. This alone is yet the most evident aspect of the experience of division that crosses the domestic church and whose consequences are also painfully tried in the choices made for the Christian education of their children.

These themes were the concerns of the first official dialogue undertaken in Italy between the Italian Episcopal Conference and the Waldensian and Methodist Churches. The study conducted by a bilateral commission that worked from 1988 to 1993 produced the *Testo comune tra cattolici e valdesi sui matrimoni misti*,[17] subsequently approved by the Synod of the Waldensian and Methodist Churches and the Italian Episcopal Conference. The text does not limit itself to the consideration of juridical matters set by these marriages but intends to offer directives of a pastoral character founded upon a theological base. For this reason, the first part of the text introduces "what as Christians we can say in common about marriage," and it delineates a brief, biblical theology of marriage, illustrating its meaning in light of creation and as sign of the covenant established by God with God's people. The second part points out the areas (the sacramentality of marriage, indissolubility, fertility) in which between Catholics and Waldensians there exist

---

a Common Understanding of the Church, Second Phase, 1984–1990, Document 66 in "XXVII. Reformed-Roman Catholic Dialogue" in Gros, Meyer, and Rusch, *Growth in Agreement II*, n. 152b, p. 815.

[17] Cf. *Testo comune di studio e di proposta per un indirizzo pastorale dei matrimoni misti [Common Study Text and Proposal for a Pastoral Address of Mixed Marriages]* in *Lettera di collegamento del Segretariato per l'ecumenismo e il dialogo della C.E.L* 32 (1 maggio 1997) 5–20.

differences of understanding or different ways of translating into action values shared by both communities.

Of particular importance are the reflections proposed by the document regarding the duty of the Christian education of children. It is necessary to take account realistically of the tensions in the fulfillment of this task coming from the different ecclesial affiliations of the couple. Therefore, respect of each one's convictions and loyalty to the discipline in force in the respective community is first of all necessary. At the same time, the parents must be charged with the responsibility of the Christian education of their children, without surrendering to the temptation to defer the option to the illusion that the church can grow in a neutral environment. If this task is assumed, the painful experience of the division among the churches can be transformed into an occasion to live reconciliation and anticipate the unity sought. This happens when the witness of the Gospel assumes the form of Christian education that has as its focus the family in its wholeness. This is possible because the existing dissension among the confessions has not destroyed consensus on the central contents of Christian faith. From this center, it is therefore possible to look for the most appropriate way for a faithful and effective transmission of the Christian message.

At times tensions arise among the issues of the ecumenical movement and among the respective ways in which to establish the priorities of the commitment to unity. In some cases the risk is present that distance among the points of view increases, even making communication impossible. Paradoxically, dialogue risks becoming impossible precisely among those who concordantly indicate it as the path to journey to reach reconciliation among the churches. Thus there is present the phenomenon of dialogue that develops spontaneously among Christians who in different churches share the same sensitivity (for example, stress placed on social commitment or the appreciation of charismatic experiences). Yet dialogue becomes difficult within churches among the different sensitivities or between the grassroots and the higher levels. In extreme cases, failed attempts of dialogue can induce people or groups to decide to follow their own way, even putting themselves in contrast with the discipline in force within the church to which they belong.

It thus happens that grassroots ecumenism is contrasted to that of higher-level ecumenism, the search for theological consensus to social commitment, and the effort to resolve the controversies of the past to attention drawn to the future. In so doing, however, one runs the risk of overcoming some divisions but creating others according to the lines that no longer coincide with the confessional confines but that are no less negative for ecclesial communion. In fact, the cause of unity is not served by creating new divisions but by looking for the most effective ways to assure coherence among the different initiatives and the ways followed in the search of the reconciliation of the churches.[18]

Endless Dialogue? The Problem of Reception

As a component of the communicative structure of the church, dialogue is destined to last as long as the church exists. In fact, it is the manifestation of ecclesial communion and the means assuring its vitality, both in its constitutive elementary form by the proclamation of the Gospel or by the profession of faith, and in its most complex and articulated forms. If this is valuable for the communicative processes at the foundation of ecclesial life, it must be asked if *ecumenical* dialogue, namely, what takes place among separated churches that intend to seek the consensus in view of the reestablishment of full communion, must be represented as a process without end.

Some respond positively to such a question, affirming that dialogue must never cease because it represents the form in which ecclesial unity finds its realization.[19] This assertion tends to distance itself from the representations of the goal of the ecumenical movement that conceive unity as absolute uniformity of church doctrine and structure. On the contrary, understood in a less rigid and static way, the unity of the church can be thought of as a dialogue aimed at the mutual recognition among ecclesial communities and the respective forms in which they express and live Christian faith.

This description of unity is plausible from the theological point of view, and it corresponds to how church history witnesses to the ways in which communion among local churches has been lived. Nevertheless, it does not mean that dialogue has to continue in the form in which it has actually developed among churches that continue to live separately. Since ecumenical dialogue has the goal to make possible the reestablishment of communion in the confession of faith, in the common celebration of the sacraments and in the exercise of ministries, once this

[18] Cf. in this regard the document published by the Institute for Ecumenical Research, Strasbourg, *Crisis and Challenge of the Ecumenical Movement: Integrity and Indivisibility* (Geneva: World Council of Churches, 1994).
[19] Cf. L. Klein, "Theologische Alternative zur Konsensökumene," in *Theologische Quartalschrift* 166 (1986) 268–78.

objective has been reached, dialogue among the churches is able to continue and must do so, but with a quality and in accord with ways different from the present ones.

Contrary to the intention of those who propose it, the premise of a dialogue destined to continue endlessly because it represents the place in which ecclesial unity is already realized could legitimate a conception of ecumenical commitment that exhausts itself in the appointment of theological commissions entrusted to discuss controversial issues without coming to some definite conclusion. In reality, theological work that unfolds in dialogue commissions has made and continues to make an essential contribution to reconciliation among the churches, but alone it is not able to reestablish full communion. Theologians place their competence at the service of the churches from which they have received their mandate, and they suggest meeting points in the expression of the faith and paths that can be responsibly pursued in the search of full communion. Judgment on the validity of the consensus in the expression of faith and on the practicability of the paths suggested, however, is up to the churches.

The question of the *reception* of ecumenical consensus surfaces at the moment of untying the knot between the activities of the commissions that conduct dialogue and the exercise of the responsibility of the churches that have conferred the mandate for dialogue. The concept of reception belongs to the history of the ancient church, and it describes the process through which the decisions of local synods and of the ecumenical councils themselves were subsequently accepted by the other churches that recognized their validity. In the context of the contemporary ecumenical movement, the same concept has been recovered for indicating the process by which the churches appropriate the consensus reached through dialogue and, on this basis, take the steps toward the reestablishment of communion.

Reception is a complex process whose outcome depends upon numerous factors. It starts off with the publication of the results of dialogue that thereby become accessible to pastors, theologians, and the faithful. Although this is not yet official reception, this aspect of the communication of the results of ecumenical dialogue must not be underestimated. In fact, the dispersal of ecumenical documents has created a new situation for theological debate. In some cases, theological reflection has already integrated significant aspects of ecumenical consensus in its own work of elaborating the contents of Christian faith. A further confirmation of the importance assumed by this element in theological debate is found in the fact that many of those who attest to confessionally rigid positions are seen forced to defend their own theological convictions by criticizing the results of ecumenical dialogue.[20] This shows that it is no longer possible to ignore ecumenical dialogue. As well, those who do theology within a homogeneous and accepted confessional context can hardly do less than compare themselves with those whom the dialogues affirm and with positions theologians of different traditions in dialogue hold as plausible expressions of the faith of their own churches. From this point of view, it can be affirmed that ecumenical dialogue has already experienced a significant reception in the theological debate that unfolds within the churches and among confessional traditions.

In the strict sense, reception of ecumenical consensus is constituted by the act by which the churches declare in an official and binding way that the results of dialogue are to be held valid, and that they allow for a reconsideration of the judgment on dissension that in the past caused separation. The official act by which the churches ratify the results of dialogue represents a fundamental passage in the process of the search of consensus. It must not be forgotten that the commissions represent the churches and act on their behalf. Ecclesial reception permits those who have conducted dialogue to verify if the solutions are acceptable on the part of the churches from whom they have received their mandate. Furthermore, judgment pronounced on matters that from time to time appear sufficiently mature for reception by the churches allows for establishing some fixed points in the gradual quest of coming closer together. In the case that it would not be possible to establish these points and to consider the acquired and determined results of dialogue, it would be difficult to think of real progress. In principle, dialogue, in fact, could always question the journey made previously and decide it is necessary to start again from the beginning.

Urgency to verify the churches' "receptibility" of consensus reached is particularly evident in the most advanced dialogues (Anglican-Roman Catholic, Lutheran-Roman Catholic). Agreement reached in them does not only concern the individual matters (justification, Eucharist, ministry); it also extends to the comprehensive ecclesial picture and to the connections that organically link together the different constitutive ele-

---

[20] This phenomenon is evident in the recent discussion taken place in Germany on the question of justification; cf. J. Baur, *Einig in Sachen Rechtfertigung? Zur Prüfung des Rechtfertigungskapitels der Studie des Ökumenischen Arbeitskreises evangelischer und katholischer Theologen: "Lehrverurteilungen–kirchentrennend"* (Tübingen: Mohr, 1989).

ments of the church. The whole construction maintains, however, a hypothetical and provisional character until its relation to the conscience of faith of the churches engaged in the dialogue is verified. In fact, the dynamism of growth internal to the dialogue is not self-sufficient; nor is it enough to give soundness to the formulated proposals, the reference to which is affirmed in preceding ecumenical documents. On the contrary, this habit could give the deceptive impression that elements only for the limited family of "ecumenists" are already to be considered securely acquired for all. Only ecclesial reception allows for overcoming the precariousness that characterizes the results of ecumenical dialogue conducted up to now.

If prolonging dialogue always makes the churches' official evaluation of its results more necessary, surely official reception of its results will proceed with extreme slowness and will seem to encounter great difficulty. Many ecumenical documents of the last years have not received a response from ecclesial authorities that have given the theological commissions their mandate. In the cases where there has been a response, this generally recognizes the validity of the fundamental affirmations of the documents submitted to the judgment of ecclesial authorities. At the same time, however, it affirms that there remain points that subsequently must be clarified, and it, therefore, recommends that the dialogue continue until such matters may be clarified in a satisfactory way. The right of the churches to freely make statements on the validity of the results of ecumenical dialogue certainly cannot be contested. It must be recognized, however, that in this way dialogue, which is approved authoritatively to continue, does not succeed in consolidating its results and overcoming the precariousness that it characterizes. Such a situation then confirms in their convictions the critics who accuse theological dialogue of being inconclusive and of representing only a façade of ecumenical engagement incapable of producing real changes in the relations among the churches.

The difficulties that prevent or slow down the reception of ecumenical dialogue depend upon many causes. There are problems tied to the ecclesial structures competent to make decisions that often must accomplish a task totally new and for which they are not equipped. In fact, it often concerns institutions that carry the signs of the historical epoch when they were born and of the tasks that have taken place for centuries. One should, then, note the complexity of decisional processes especially in those churches which, unlike the Roman Catholic Church, do not have central bodies of magisterium but come to decisions through the effort to make emerge a consensus of a synodical character. The same form in which the results of ecumenical dialogue have been given back to the churches has not always been most appropriate for obtaining a response to the issues posed. The breadth of the texts, their heterogeneous character, and the weight of historical-theological analysis have made it difficult to formulate a clear and binding response that was judged necessary. Finally, as for the criterion of judgment to be employed in the evaluation of the results of dialogue, it is not at all easy to delimit with clarity the setting of the necessary unity in faith and that of the legitimate pluralism in the expression of faith and in ecclesial structures. In some cases, the official evaluation of ecumenical texts gives the impression that, despite the declarations to the contrary, the goal of dialogue in fact continues to be conceived as reaching something totally identical in the formulation of doctrine.

The signing of the *Joint Declaration on the Doctrine of Justification* by the Catholic Church and the Lutheran churches (October 31, 1999) represents a case of ecclesial reception of the results of an ecumenical dialogue completed with success. The exhausting process of editing the document and the turmoil that accompanied the churches' discussion revealed the difficulties that official reception encounters but also that such difficulties are not insuperable. In this case, the editing of a brief text, which intended to summarize the results of the dialogue on justification conducted in the preceding decades, has allowed for official affirmation that "a consensus in the basic truths of the doctrine of justification" (*Joint Declaration* 40) exists between the Catholic Church and the Lutheran churches. On the basis of such a consensus, which is also able to support differences remaining in the manner of interpreting justification, it is possible to declare that the mutual condemnations of the sixteenth century do not apply to the doctrine presented in the declaration.

Beyond the importance the theme of justification has in relations between the Catholic Church and the Reformation churches, the text has great significance because it might be able to assume an exemplary character for the reception of theological consensus and to indicate a viable method for other settings. In fact, the *Joint Declaration* represents the successful attempt to go beyond the accumulative quantity of consensus documents that characterize the present ecumenical moment by trying to confer a more authoritative and recognized *status* of consensus reached through dialogue. In this way, dialogue may also continue to construct itself upon a more solid foundation.

A correct evaluation of the time factor is essential in the process of ecumenical consensus. On one hand, dialogue cannot go on endlessly, but it demands verification of the validity of how much has been achieved. On the other hand, wanting to restrict time, pretending the reception of a consensus not yet sufficiently mature, risks jeopardizing the outcome of the entire process. If the impatience of a person who has the impression that the dialogues do not modify ecclesial relations in a profound way is comprehensible, it must also be remembered that the breaches that were perpetrated in a distant past and that settled in the life of the churches over centuries cannot be eliminated in the blink of an eye: "The ecumenical task is enormous and we have to adopt a time-scale appropriate to the scale of the problems. On that proper scale, the setbacks look like small interruptions and not major disasters."[21]

Dialogue and Recognition

At the end of our exploration, we want to return to the matter mentioned at the beginning of the chapter: what are the implications of the choice of the method of dialogue for the individuals so involved? To answer this question it is necessary to state more directly the ecclesiological significance of dialogue and to specify if and to what point whether what is good for human dialogue in general finds an exact correspondence in the dialogue among the churches. The matter is not exactly superfluous or without concrete consequences. For example, it concerns establishing whether the necessity to recognize the individuals in dialogue as interlocutors with equal dignity and rights can be transferred in a pure and simple way to the level of relations among the churches. In this case, the decision to undertake dialogue and its realization must be considered equivalent to the recognition of the Christian community with which one enters dialogue as an authentic and full realization of the church of Christ to which must be attributed the same value of one's own church. A conclusion of this kind is considered unacceptable even by many churches actively engaged in ecumenical dialogue. In the first chapter, we recalled how respect for ecclesiological convictions and for the judgment each churches makes on the ecclesial worth of other communities has constituted the necessary presupposition for the dialogue that goes on within the WCC.

On the other hand, dialogue cannot be considered a neutral instrument for use in the search of a solution to problems of a doctrinal or

---

[21] G. R. Evans, *Method in Ecumenical Theology*, 5–6.

other carefully circumscribed character. It is always the personal encounter and, in the case of ecumenical dialogue, the encounter of the churches, that, in greater or smaller measure, has as consequence a transformation of the individuals involved in it. Despite the common work concentrating on the dissension to overcome it, dialogue has a scope with a more far-reaching character, and it creates the conditions to reconsider the judgments of the interlocutors. In the eyes of the Catholic who is seriously committed in dialogue, the Protestant no longer appears simply as "one who refuses to recognize the supremacy of the pope, who denies five sacraments out of seven, who refuses to recognize the Virgin Mary, but is a Christian who lives by many positive values in Christianity, and who, ever since the sixteenth century, has been developing these values."[22] Along this line is the teaching of Vatican II which, before enumerating the issues to be faced through theological dialogue, points out the elements the Catholic Church has in common with other churches and ecclesial communities and that constitute the real though imperfect communion existing among them.

Nevertheless, it must be noted that in Vatican II the foundation of dialogue takes place in a perspective more anthropological than ecclesiological. According to the decree *Unitatis Redintegratio*, through dialogue it is possible to acquire "a truer knowledge and more just appreciation of the teaching of the life of each communion"; in addition, dialogue helps "promote justice and truth, concord and collaboration, as well as the spirit of love and unity" (*UR* 4). Dialogue represents, therefore, an effective means by which to overcome prejudices and misunderstandings and to enable the best mutual knowledge among different ecclesial communities. Dialogue thus appears to be the most suitable method for a search of the truth that occurs with respect to liberty and human dignity.

However, an explicit ecclesiological justification of dialogue with other churches is not found in Vatican II: "Dialogue is not discussed in the light of its possible principles, but rather is accepted on the grounds of well-tested ecumenical methodology."[23] Also, the principle enunciated in the Decree on Ecumenism, according to which dialogue has been realized on the level of parity *(par cum pari)* among participants,[24]

---

[22] Y. Congar, *Ecumenism and the Future of the Church*, 29.

[23] J. E. Vercruysse, "Is Dialogue Acceptable from an Ecclesiological Point of View? A Catholic View," in *Les dialogues oecuméniques hier et aujourd'hui* (Les études théologiques de Chambésy) (Chambésy: Centre Orthodoxe, 1985) 358.

[24] "Most valuable for this purpose are meetings of the two sides—especially for discussion of theological problems—where each side can treat with the other on an equal

does not say anything about the ecclesial *status* of the interlocutor with whom from time to time the Catholic Church enters in relationship. Conducting dialogue remains in the setting of procedural and methodological refinement.[25]

If the choice of dialogue as an adequate way to seek unity is not explicitly motivated in ecclesial terms, then it cannot deny that Vatican II contains the elements that can allow establishing this connection. Practical indications about the attitude to assume toward other ecclesial communities must in fact be read within the general ecclesiological frame proposed by Vatican II. We have already recalled how, from an ecclesiological point of view, overcoming a simplistic identification of the church of Christ with the Catholic Church has been a decisive element in accepting the ecumenical movement. If outside the visible body of the Catholic Church are found "elements of sanctification and of truth" that belong to the church of Christ but are so interconnected that they form "churches and ecclesial communities," it is natural that with these bodies that derive their identity from the same mystery of which the Catholic Church lives, it must establish dialogue. The "ecclesial elements" in virtue of which a real communion is given between the Catholic Church and other Christian churches do not only make dialogue possible but they impose it so that it might be possible to put an end to contradictory situations in which the churches find themselves due to the lack of full communion. It can, therefore, be affirmed that, beyond the way the choice of dialogue is justified, an objective connection exists between the direction of the dialogical method from Vatican II as a way to rediscover unity and the vision of the church that is proposed.

More than thirty years since the conclusion of Vatican II, clarification of the ecclesiological significance of dialogue is respected for another reason: the real experience of ecumenical dialogue conducted by the Catholic Church has known a development that has gone well

---

footing, provided that those who take part in them under the guidance of their authorities are truly competent" (*UR* 9).

[25] This has been precisely stressed on the Protestant side: "When the Vatican II Decree on Ecumenism spoke of coming dialogues 'on equal footing' (*par cum pari*), many Protestants greeted this as a historic acknowledgment of the ecclesial equality of separated churches, not realising that the principle referred primarily to a ground rule of ecumenical ethics and etiquette without which no dialogue would thrive. The ground rule is indispensable precisely because of the dissimilarity of the partners," Nils Ehrenström and Günther Gaßmann, *Confessions in Dialogue: A Survey of Bilateral Conversations among World Confessional Families 1959–1974*, Third, revised and enlarged edition by Nils Ehrenström (Faith and Order Paper 63) (Geneva: World Council of Churches, 1975) 246.

beyond what the council had ever imagined. The Decree on Ecumenism's supposition was that primarily a dialogue would unfold among private theologians under the surveillance of pastors. Yet, in reality, the postconciliar period has seen the Catholic Church engaged in numerous official dialogues with mainline Christian communions. Nevertheless, on the level of ecclesiological reflection, sufficient attention has not yet been given to these developments. What significance must be attributed to the fact that, despite Catholic reservations about the ministries existing in the Reformation churches, the heads of these churches would be recognized by the Catholic Church as legitimate representatives of these communities, qualified to speak on their behalf. Is the term "churches," attributed in the dialogues to the communities of the Reformation, only representative of the way they define themselves, or does it imply a theological recognition and a newness regarding the formula "ecclesial community" used by Vatican II?

The praxis of dialogue could have anticipated the elements that have not yet been adequately considered in the elaboration of theory on the church. Or, on the contrary, it could reveal positions needing correction because they are incompatible with the Catholic understanding of the church. In any case, it does not deal with facts deprived of importance for the awareness that the Catholic Church has of its own identity and of relations it has with other churches. An ineluctable task for ecclesiological reflection is, therefore, a careful and critical evaluation of the implicit content in the experience of ecumenical dialogue.

The praxis affirmed in the relationships among the churches is certainly liable of different interpretations. Therefore, it is not helpful to overload with theological meaning and interpret in a tendentious way expressions and ways of acting that do not have a univocal sense. But neither can everything be reduced to a simple etiquette that has nothing to say on the level of recognition of the ecclesial character of the interlocutor. The ecclesiological picture of Vatican II, which has enabled the development of these ecumenical relations, must be the subject of a reflection that proceeds before integrating new data the dialogue has been given to discover.[26]

The necessity to respond to the questions mentioned and to clarify the implications of dialogue is particularly evident on the occasion of the official reception of a dialogue. Symptomatic to this intention

---

[26] Cf. the interesting perspectives of methodological character contained in the article of W. Kasper, "Das Zweite Vatikanum weiterdenken. Die apostolische Sukzession im Bischofsamt als ökumenisches Problem," in *Kerygma und Dogma* 44 (1998) 207–18.

is a passage of the process that has brought Catholics and Lutherans to sign the *Joint Declaration on the Doctrine of Justification*. After having expressed its appreciation for the effort achieved by the Lutheran World Federation to reach a shared position through the consultation of synods, the Catholic response of June 1998 observes that "the question of the real authority of such a synodical consensus, today and also tomorrow, in the life and doctrine of the Lutheran community" remains unresolved.[27] The observation contained in the Vatican document has aroused reactions of disappointment, and it has given birth to the suspicion that might place in question from the Catholic side the reliability of the Lutheran churches at the moment in which they make their official statement on the consensus reached. The Catholic side has subsequently specified the meaning of its affirmation and confirmed its respect for the decisional procedures followed by the Lutheran World Federation.[28] Nevertheless, there remains the substantial matter that cannot be reduced to an incident due to an unfortunate formulation.

Ecumenical dialogue develops in a situation through many paradoxical aspects. On one hand, the recognition of the ecclesial quality of the interlocutor is a necessary presupposition to be able to undertake dialogue. In fact, ecumenical dialogue cannot be compared to diplomatic relations the Catholic Church maintains with some states. Rather, it is about a process through which it is intended to reach such a common expression of faith that allows the reestablishment of full ecclesial communion. From the ecclesiological point of view, this presupposes that already in separation there is at least a certain homogeneity among the interlocutors and that they consider reliable the witness of faith made by their counterparts. In fact, it would be contradictory to look for consensus of faith with an interlocutor who is not considered worthy of trust when giving witness to the faith. On the other hand, it is equally evident that there are differences, even deep ones, in the way of conceiving the church. Such differences lead to the Catholic position to

[27] Congregation for the Doctrine of the Faith and the Pontifical Council for Promoting Christian Unity (Doctrinal Congregation, Unity Council/Justification), "Official Catholic Response to Joint Declaration" in *Origins* 28:8 (July 16, 1998) n. 6, p. 131.

[28] The significance affirmed in the Catholic response is clarified in an annex to the Joint Declaration: "The response of the Catholic Church response does not intend to put in question the authority of Lutheran Synods or of the Lutheran World Federation. The Catholic Church and the Lutheran World Federation began the dialogue and have taken it forward as partners with equal rights *(par cum pari)*. Notwithstanding different conceptions of authority in the church, each partner respects the other partner's ordered process of reaching doctrinal decisions." In *Reseptio* 1/1999 (15.6.1999) n. 4, p. 6.

retain that the church in its fullness is not realized in communities with which it undertakes dialogue.

The tension is intensified when the dialogical process reaches the point where it is necessary to take a qualitative step forward and to verify whether the consensus reached can be received by the churches. The act by which the churches receive and ratify consensus could indeed be considered from the point of view of the subject on which judgment is pronounced. They affirm that the formulation of faith and the theological explanation which declares that the dissension of the past is overcome are corresponding, or at least compatible, with their own faith. The same act, however, can also be considered from the point of view of the individuals who make it. From this perspective, one cannot be in disagreement with the Catholic response to the *Joint Declaration on the Doctrine of Justification* when it states that Catholics and Lutherans have different understandings of the magisterial authority of the church. Nevertheless, as such differences did not prevent the fruitful carrying out of dialogue, so neither did they necessarily prevent ratifying its results. This act can be responsibly taken on the basis of the elements that found the already existing communion, and at the same time it broadens this basis because it recognizes the validity of the consensus reached and declares the condemnations of the past no longer apply to how the churches today declare their belief.

Ecumenical dialogue does not, therefore, allow itself to be removed from the described tensions, but it anticipates already, although in a provisional and "experimental" way, the conditions of communion it intends to make possible. It reveals a dynamism that, from the initial recognition of the churches that undertake dialogue, tends toward an ever fuller recognition. Dialogue allows for the recognition of evangelical authenticity which the interlocutor has always considered its peculiar characteristic, together with its errors and limits. The final goal of dialogue is to come, through the recognition that permits accepting different ways to live and express the one faith, to the full mutual recognition of the churches.

Bibliography

Acerbi, A., ed. *Il ministero del Papa in prospettiva ecumenica*. Milano: Vita e Pensiero, 1999. (collection of essays comparing the findings of the dialogues between the Roman Catholic Church and other churches on the ministry of unity for the universal church)

Bell, G.K.A. *Christian Unity: The Anglican Position*. London: Hodder & Stoughton, 1948. (classical presentation of the Anglican position on unity, proposed by one of the authoritative figures of the history of the ecumenical movement)

Best, T. and Robra, M., eds. *Ecclesiology and Ethics. Ecumenical Ethical Engagement, Moral Formation and the Nature of the Church*. Geneva: World Council of Churches, 1997. (collection of recent documents of the WCC on the relationship between ecclesiology and ethics)

Cereti, G. *Molte chiese cristiane un'unica chiesa di Cristo: Corso di Ecumenismo*. Brescia: Queriniana, 199. (introduction to the main themes of ecumenical history and theology)

_____. *Riforma della chiesa e unità dei cristiani nell'insegnamento del Concilio Vaticano II*. Verona: Il Segno, 1985. (study on the theme of church reform in *Unitatis Redintegratio*)

Cereti, Giovanni e Puglisi, James F., a cura di. *Enchiridion Œcumenicum. Documenti del dialogo teologico interconfessionale 3: Dialoghi internazionali 1985–1994*. Bologna: Edizioni Dehoniane, 1995.

_____. *Enchiridion Œcumenicum. Documenti del dialogo teologico interconfessionale 4: Dialoghi locali 1988–1994*. Bologna: Edizioni Dehoniane, 1996.

Chenu, B. *La signification ecclésiologique du Conseil Oecuménique des Églises 1945–1963*. Paris: Beauchesne, 1972. (ecclesiological study on the nature of the WCC in light of the debate which accompanied its foundation)

Congar, Y. *Dialogue between Christians: Catholic Contributions to Ecumenism*. West-minster, Md.: Newman Press, 1966. (English translation of *Chrétiens en dia-logue: contributions catholiques à l'œcuménisme* [Unam Sanctam 50] Paris: Édi-tions du Cerf, 1964. (collection of essays related to the ecumenical activity of the author during the pre-Vatican II conciliar period)

_____. *Diversity and Communion*. Mystic, Conn.: Twenty-Third Publications, 1984. (English translation of *Diversités et communion: dossier historique et conclusion théologique*. [Cogitatio Fidei 112] Paris: Éditions du Cerf, 1982). (collection of essays that document the post-Vatican II conciliar reflection of the author)

_____. *Divided Christendom: A Catholic Study of the Problem of Reunion*. London: Geoffrey Bles, 1939 (English translation of *Chrétiens désunis: principes d'un œcuménisme catholique* [Unam Sanctam 1] Paris: Éditions du Cerf, 1937). (classical work that inaugurates Catholic ecumenism).

Dick, J. A. *The Malines Conversations Revisited*. (Bibliotheca Ephemeridum Theo-logicarum Lovaniensium 85). Leuven/Louvain, Belgium: Leuven Univer-sity Press/Presses Universitaires de Louvain (Uitgeverij Peeters, 1989. (ac-curate reconstruction of the Malines Conversations)

Ehrenström, N. and Gaßmann, G. *Confessions in Dialogue: A Survey of Bilateral Conversations among World Confessional Families 1959–1974*. Third, revised, and enlarged edition by N. Ehrenström. (Faith and Order Paper 63). Ge-neva: World Council of Churches, 1975. (review of ecumenical bilateral dia-logues and a comparative analysis of their themes and methods)

Enchiridion Oecumenicum. Documenti del dialogo teologico interconfessionale voll. I–IV. Bologna, EDB, 1986–1996. (compilation of the principal documents of international and local ecumenical dialogue)

Evans, G. R. *Method in Ecumenical Theology: The Lessons So Far*. Cambridge: Cambridge University Press, 1996. (study on the theological method ap-plied in the dialogues)

Fey, H. E., ed. *A History of the Ecumenical Movement, Volume 2: The Ecumenical Advance 1948–1968*. Geneva: World Council of Churches, 1993[3]. (continua-tion of the history of the ecumenical movement of R. Rouse and S. C. Neil)

Fouilloux, E. *Les catholiques et l'unite chrétienne du XIXe au XXe siècle. Itinérai-res européens d'expression française*. Paris: Centurion, 1982. (analytical study of the Catholic positions in the French context concerning the problem of unity and the shift from unionism to ecumenism)

Fries, H. and Rahner, K. *Unity of the Churches: An Actual Possibility*. Philadel-phia: Fortress Press, 1985. (English translation of *Einigung der Kirchen—re-ale Möglichkeit*. Freiburg im Breisgau: Verlag Herder, 1983). (proposal by two theologians of practical ways toward church unity; it evoked lively discussion)

Gassmann, G. *Konzeptionen der Einheit in der Bewegung für Glauben und Kirchenverfassung 1910–1937*, Vandenhoeck & Ruprecht, Göttingen, 1979. (study on the ways to conceive the goal of the ecumenical movement in the first phases of Faith and Order)

Gros, J., F.S.C., Meyer, H., and Rusch, W. G., eds. *Growth in Agreement II: Reports and Agreed Statements of Ecumenical Conversations on a World Level 1982–1998*. (Faith and Order Paper 187). Grand Rapids, MI/Geneva: Eerdmans Publishing Company/World Council of Churches, 2000. (Volume based on Meyer, H., Urban, H. G., und Vischer, L., Hrsg. *Dokumente wachsender Übereinstimmung II: 1982–1990*, Padeborn/Frankfurt am Main: Bonifatius GmbH Verlag/Verlag Otto Lembeck, 1992.)

Limouris, G. ed. *Orthodox Visions of Ecumenism. Statements, Messages and Reports on the Ecumenical Movement 1902–1992*, WCC, Geneva, 1994. (collection of official documents of the Orthodox churches on the ecumenical movement)

Lossky, N. and others, eds. *Dictionary of the Ecumenical Movement* (First Edition). Geneva/Grand Rapids, Mich.: World Council of Churches/Eerdmans Publishing Company, 1991. (basic source for the themes and prominent figures of the ecumenical movement)

_____. *Dictionary of the Ecumenical Movement* (Second Edition). Geneva: World Council of Churches, 2002. (basic source for the themes and prominent figures of the ecumenical movement)

Maffeis, A. *Giustificazione. Percorsi teologici nel dialogo tra le chiese*. Cinisello Balsamo (MI): Edizioni Paoline, 1998. (presentation of the issue of justification, of the factors that enabled the dialogue to begin and to reach a remarkable consensus)

_____. *Il ministero nella chiesa: uno studio del dialogo cattolico-luterano (1967–1984)*. (Pontificia Università Gregoriana: Dissertatio Series Romana 2). Gorgonzola, Milano: Glossa, 1991. (study on the first two phases of the Lutheran-Roman Catholic international dialogue with particular attention to the themes of ordained ministry and ecclesiology)

Meyer, H. and Vischer, L., eds. *Growth in Agreement: Reports and Agreed Statements of Ecumenical Conversations on a World Level* [Volume I, 1971–1982, with one Anglican-Old Catholic statement from 1931; there are errors and omissions in the endnotes]. (Ecumenical Documents II/Faith and Order Paper 108). New York/Geneva: Paulist Press/World Council of Churches, 1984.

Neuner, P. *Teologia Ecumenica. La ricerca dell'unità tra le chiese cristiane*. (Biblioteca di teologia contemporanea 110). Brescia: Queriniana, 2000. (Italian translation of *Ökumenische Theologie. Die Suche nach der Einheit der christlichen*

Kirchen. Darmstadt: Wissenschaftliche Buchgesellschaft, 1997). (complete presentation of the principal historical and theological aspects of the ecumenical movement)

Pattaro, G. *Corso di teologla dell'ecumenismo.* Brescia: Queriniana, 1985. (reflections on the question of unity among the churches by one of Italy's ecumenical pioneers)

Raiser, K. *Ecumenism in Transition: A Paradigm Shift in the Ecumenical Movement?* Geneva: World Council of Churches, 1991. (English translation of *Ökumene im Übergang: Paradigmenwechsel in der ökumenischen Bewegung?* München: Christian Kaiser Verlag, 1989). (introduction by a General Secretary of the WCC to theological paradigm shift that is being made in the ecumenical movement)

Rouse, R. and Neill, S. C., eds. *A History of the Ecumenical Movement, 1517–1948.* [Volume 1]. Geneva: World Council of Churches, 1993⁴. (classical reconstruction of the history of the ecumenical movement promoted by the WCC)

Sartori, L. *L'unità delle Chiese: un dibattito e un progetto.* Brescia: Queriniana, 1989. (presentation of the debate on ecclesial models of unity)

_____. *Teologia ecumenica. Saggi.* Padova: Gregoriana, 1987. (collection of essays on various aspects of the ecumenical problem)

Schmidt, S. *Augustine Bea: The Cardinal of Unity.* New York: New City Press, 1987. (biography of Cardinal Bea, first president of the Secretariat for Promoting Christian Unity)

Sesboüé, B. *Pour une théologie œcuménique: Église et sacrements, Eucharistie et ministères, La Vierge Marie.* (Cogitatio Fidei 160). Paris: Éditions du Cerf, 1990. (collection of essays on central themes of ecumenical theology)

Sgarbossa, R. *La Chiesa come mistero di comunione nei documenti del dialogo internazionale luterano-cattolico (1967–1984).* (Dissertatio ad Doctoratum in Facultate Theologiae Pontificiae Universitatis Gregorianae). Padova: Messaggero di S. Antonio Editrice, 1994. (study on the ecclesiology of the Lutheran-Roman Catholic international dialogue)

Tavard, G. *Petite histoire du mouvement oecuménique.* Paris: Fleurus, 1960. (history of the ecumenical movement with particular attention to the Roman Catholic position)

Thils, G. *Histoire doctrinale du mouvement œcuménique.* (Bibliotheca Ephemeridum Theologicarum Lovaniensium 8). (Nouvelle édition). Louvain: E. Warny [1962]. (critical presentation by a Roman Catholic theologian of the themes discussed in the ecumenical movement)

Thurian, M., ed. *Churches Respond to Baptism, Eucharist and Ministry: Official Responses to the "Baptism, Eucharist and Ministry" Text. Volumes I–VI.* (Faith and Order Papers 129, 132, 135, 137, 143, 144). Geneva: World Council of Churches, 1986–1988. (collection of the churches' responses to the Lima document on baptism, Eucharist and ministry)

Tillard, J.-M. *Church of Churches: The Ecclesiology of Communion*. Collegeville, Minn.: Liturgical Press/A Michael Glazier Book, 1992. (English translation of *Église d'Églises: L'ecclésiologie de communion*. [Cogitatio Fidei 143]. Paris: Éditions du Cerf, 1987). (resumption of the ecclesiological vision, founded on the notion of communion, of one of the Catholic theologians who has most recently influenced ecumenical dialogue)

Urban, H.-J. und Wagner, H., Hrsg. *Handbuch der Ökumenik*. (Im Auftrag des J.-A.-Möhler-Instituts). Bände I–III/2. Paderborn: Verlag Bonifatius-Druckerei, 1985–1987. (extensive and intense presentation of the historical and theological aspects of the ecumenical movement)

Velati, M. *Una difficile transizione. Il cattolicesimo tra unionismo ed ecumenismo (1952–1964)*. Bologna: Il Mulino, 1996. (reconstruction of the activity of the Catholic Conference for Ecumenical Questions in the period preceeding the Second Vatican Council and the emergence of the Secretariat for the Unity of the Christians)

Vercruysse, J. *Introduzione alla teologia ecumenica*. (Introduzione alle Discipline Teologiche 11). Casale Monferrato (AL): Edizioni Piemme, 1992. (introduction to the principal themes of the history and theology of the ecumenical movement)

Visser 't Hooft, W. A. *The Genesis and Formation of the World Council of the Churches*. Geneva: World Council of Churches, 1987[2]. (accurate reconstruction of the process of formation of the WCC, of which he was the first General Secretary)

Voicu, Sever J. e Cereti, Giovanni, a cura di. *Enchiridion Œcumenicum. Documenti del dialogo teologico interconfessionale 1: Dialoghi internazionali 1931–1984*. Bologna: Edizioni Dehoniane, 1986.

_____. *Enchiridion Œcumenicum. Documenti del dialogo teologico interconfessionale 2: Dialoghi locali 1965–1987*. Bologna: Edizioni Dehoniane, 1988.

Zizioulas, J. *L'être ecclésial*. Genève: Labor et Fides, 1981. (collection of essays of one of the most influential orthodox theologians in recent ecumenical dialogue)